John Pritchard is Bishop of Oxford and Chairman of the Church of England Board of Education. He was formerly Bishop of Jarrow, Archdeacon of Canterbury and, before that, Warden of Cranmer Hall, Durham. He has served in parishes in Birmingham and Taunton, and has been Diocesan Youth Officer for Bath and Wells diocese. Other books by the author include *The Intercessions Handbook, The Second Intercessions Handbook, Beginning Again, How to Pray, Living Easter Through the Year, How to Explain Your Faith, The Life and Work of a Priest, Going to Church, Living Jesus* and *God Lost and Found*. He is married to Wendy and has two married daughters.

D1389976

LIVING FAITHFULLY

Following Christ in everyday life

John Pritchard

First published in Great Britain in 2013

Society for Promoting Christian Knowledge
36 Causton Street
London SW1P 4ST
www.spckpublishing.co.uk

British Library Cataloguing-in-Publication Data
A catalogue record for this book is available from the British Library

ISBN 978–0–281–06762–6
eBook ISBN 978–0–281–06763–3

Typeset by Graphicraft Limited, Hong Kong
First printed in Great Britain by Ashford Colour Press
Subsequently digitally printed in Great Britain

Produced on paper from sustainable forests

Contents

—◆◆◆—

Contents

A word at the beginning

What does it mean to follow Jesus in everyday life? It's a pretty basic question but one with which we struggle. We know what it is to run churches, offer worship, raise money (endlessly) and organize everything from flower festivals to children's holiday clubs. But how does all this relate to the issues we face as we walk through the door of our office or school or hospital? How does it have any bearing on how we spend our money or conduct our marriage? How does it help us handle our sexuality or live in an online jungle?

This book emerges out of a lifelong frustration that in the Church we spend huge amounts of time tending our back garden and not enough time on the streets. Much of the energy of church life is swallowed up by an understandable concern to secure our buildings, finances and structures. We know that the purpose of it all is out there on the streets where ordinary life is going on regardless, but it's very hard to relate the domesticity of the back garden to the complexity and sheer messiness of street life.

I'm as guilty as anyone of this imbalance. But I continue to be driven by the conviction that 'God so loved the world' that he came to the world, died in the world and rose for the world. The Church is a wonderful and absorbing gift, but it shouldn't be the main focus of our concern. So how can we more effectively relate Sunday worship to Monday life? How can we close that gap and step out more confidently into the week, knowing that the Christian faith has far more to contribute to the welfare of society than society thinks? How can we help each other discover the exhilaration of living faithfully on the streets?

A word at the beginning

The Diocese of Oxford has had a strategic framework called Living Faith in which we have tried to explore what discipleship looks like in everyday terms. This book is a contribution to that process, dedicated with affection to the clergy and laity of that fascinating diocese, but it's intended to offer a much wider readership a 'starter kit' on a whole range of issues we all face as soon as we leave the safety of church on Sunday morning. For each chapter, I've included a section entitled 'Taking it further', in the hope that it may lead to stimulating discussion in church groups. That's where the real engagement might take place.

As ever my thanks go to Alison Barr, my loyal and talented editor, to Wendy, my patient wife and lifelong friend, to my team in the office – Amanda Bloor, Christine Lodge and Debbie Perry – who defend my space, and to all those whose way of living faithfully has inspired my thinking.

This book is only an introduction, but the question of how to follow Christ in daily life, Monday to Saturday, is both urgent and full of fascination.

John Pritchard

The case for the prosecution

'Religion is what an individual does with his solitariness.'[1] So said philosopher Alfred North Whitehead, and many of us have been only too keen to agree. The trouble is we've been wrong, and the consequences for the Christian faith have been disastrous.

Christianity is a public faith, lived out in specific actions. Indeed, Christianity is a verb before it's a noun. The problem, however, is that people of faith love to hunker down in subdued lighting and think about God and the universe; emptying the bins and doing the washing up just doesn't have the same attraction. We follow a man who seems to have spent the entire three years of his ministry outdoors and in public, but we have a preference for reflection, private prayer and house groups. I exaggerate, of course; Jesus spent hours in prayer, and Christians do huge amounts of good in their communities, but I want to highlight the problem clearly.

The issue goes deep. See if the following makes sense.

What's the problem?

A group of well-meaning and sincere people once had an overwhelming experience of God. It was so vivid and extraordinary that they immediately wanted to mark the place where it had happened so that they, and generations after them, would have a permanent reminder of the time and place that God had appeared to them. So they placed a stone in the ground. Soon, however, they felt the need to honour this special place more adequately, so they put up a building, modest but distinctive, so that others too would know how special this place was.

The group of people didn't want to leave the Special Place because it meant so much to them. Moreover, they developed a range of rituals appropriate to such a Special Place; you couldn't treat it as if it were an ordinary room where you left the dirty washing on the floor and forgot to make the bed. You needed to move with dignity, to acknowledge particular parts of the building, and to speak with care. Indeed, they developed a use of language that was rich, refined and somewhat obscure, in order to demonstrate, again, that this was a Special Place, and if you came in here you should not expect normal human interactions, but rather a specialized form of human behaviour appropriate to the memory of the divine presence.

Inevitably, in time, the Special Place came to be seen as the domain of God and the area outside the walls as the domain of not-God. The holiness associated with the presence of God could only be guaranteed within the walls of the building. Outside – well, 'there be dragons'. God might or might not be active out there but, if he was, it would obviously be in a much diluted form. In any case, there was so much nastiness and corruption beyond the high walls of the Special Place it was best not to go there too much.

Hence the emergence of the Church's great heresy – the sacred–secular divide. This is the dualism that has crippled the Church's mission since the time of Constantine. It's the spiritual crime that has often tried to imprison Christ in his Church when the Great Lion of God has been wanting to roam the world. These are some of the consequences:

- Good Christians have been confined to barracks instead of being released as frontline missioners in their daily lives.
- The world of work, where most people spend so much time and where much of their identity is shaped, is often unrecognized and undervalued in church life and teaching.
- Little time and resource is offered to support Christians in relating their faith to their daily lives and the complex personal and ethical decisions they have to make there.

- The Christian faith is not brought sufficiently into relationship with a whole range of social and psychological factors that shape our lives, from politics and finance to sexuality and science.
- Christians are left with schizophrenic lives, experienced as sincere faith in the personal sphere and confused secularism in the public sphere. For one hour a week (in church) the focus is clear; for the other 167 hours in the week you're on your own.
- Believers are expected to come to church on a Sunday as empty receptacles, ready and waiting to be filled, and without a distinctive identity as a secondary teacher, a bank employee, a carer, a volunteer at the Citizens Advice Bureau and so on.
- What we've followed during the week in the news about welfare reform, the pensions crisis, tax evasion, the Higgs boson particle, corruption in high places and other issues, is unmentioned and unmentionable, somehow off-limits, even to a gospel of global transformation.
- Followers of Jesus are recruited to be church officials and servers, lesson readers and cleaners of the brass, choristers and committee members – good causes all, but not the world-changing witnesses Jesus seems to have had in mind when he commissioned his little group of friends on a misty morning in Galilee to 'go and make disciples of all nations' (Matthew 28.19).

This is not just the experience of the faithful Christian in the pew. It's the experience of this bishop as well. The Church is a greedy master. Its centripetal forces drag me into church-related activity time and again when I would love to be out where I believe the centrifugal force of the gospel wants me to go. And sadly I'm not innocent in this. I collude with the seductive belief that the Church needs me to sort out its problems before I can set out from the Special Place. Just a bit more work and all will be well, and then I can get on with the real job. The devil laughs.

By now, faith is more or less burned into me. It's the core of my being, even if I fail, all the time, to live up to my calling as a follower of Christ. Nevertheless, I try constantly to remind myself that a living faith makes a difference to the world both within me (what I call spirituality) and around me (what I call discipleship). This book is about how the first makes a difference to the second and how the second makes a difference to the first.

How could we think about this?

A key text might be the words of C. S. Lewis: 'I believe in God as I believe the sun has risen, not only because I see it, but because by it I see everything else.'[2] Because of my faith I see everything differently: not just the safe 'religious things', but everything. By the light of faith I should be able to understand and evaluate *Christianly* what's going on in my own life, my family life, my workplace, my friendships, my leisure pursuits, the way I spend my money and so on. I should also be able to respond *as a Christian* to my social and political commitments, to the culture I inhabit and to the news I imbibe, to the major ethical debates of the time and the current intellectual challenges to faith. 'By it [belief in God] I see everything else.'

When I talk to groups about discipleship in daily life I often bring out an orange and start peeling it.[3] I suggest that our Christian lives are a bit like the segments of the orange: we offer to God those segments labelled 'going to church', 'praying and reading the Bible' (however intermittently), 'being on the church council' (or other such worthwhile activity), 'giving' (what we think we can afford). But then I point to all the other segments that somehow we keep to ourselves as if God isn't interested in them or we aren't interested in offering them to him. So God doesn't get a look at ethics in the workplace, stress, politics, sexuality, shopping, hobbies, sport, temptation, celebrity gossip, soap operas and so on. It's not that we're deeply resistant to the idea that all this is also related to God; it's just never really occurred to us to let Christ into those areas of life.

By contrast, I then pick up an apple and with a determined crunch bite my way into that unsegmented fruit. This is a better model for discipleship, I suggest. An apple isn't divided up into separate parts. It's whole and consistent, the only variation being where some part has got bruised or otherwise damaged. In the same way, following Christ is a whole-life commitment. Some parts of our discipleship may be bruised but Jesus came to address every aspect of our lives with his transforming message. Paul said:

> I appeal to you . . . brothers and sisters, to present your bodies [that is, your whole lives] as a living sacrifice, holy and acceptable to God, which is your spiritual worship. Do not be conformed to this world, but be transformed by the renewing of your minds.   (Romans 12.1–2)

If you'll excuse the simplicity, discipleship is about being an apple rather than an orange.

What could we do differently?

There is, however, another side to the somewhat depressing picture I've painted of faith being unconnected to everyday realities. The fact is that many Christians get on with trying to make a difference in their communities, often without making a conscious connection with their Christian faith. 'It's just what you do,' they might say. At a semi-conscious level they know their faith is a motivating factor, but that link is just as likely to be downplayed on the grounds of modesty. The British don't wear their faith on their sleeves. The link might also simply be unrecognized because it's not been made in the teaching they've received at their church, from Sunday School, through confirmation, to Sunday sermons. Nevertheless, they get on with loving their neighbour and building community.

In 2000 the Harvard sociologist Robert Putnam published a much-read book called *Bowling Alone*[4] in which he recounted the story of the loss of community in the United States, using the evocative image of people bowling alone in the nation's bowling alleys, rather than in clubs. However, in 2010 he published a second book called *American Grace*[5] in which he describes his discovery that community and what is often called 'social capital' is actually alive and well in one place more than any other in America, and that is in the nation's places of worship. Jonathan Sacks offers this précis:

> If you are a regular church or synagogue attendee, you are more likely to give money to charity . . . You are also more likely to do voluntary work for a charity, give money to a homeless person, give excess change back to a shop assistant, donate blood, help a neighbour with their shopping, spend time with someone who is depressed, allow another driver to cut in front of you, offer a seat to a stranger or help someone find a job. It goes further than this: frequent worshippers are also more active citizens . . . They take a more active part in local civic life, from local elections to town meetings to demonstrations. They are disproportionately represented among local activists for social and political reform. They turn up, they get involved, they lead.[6]

There is, therefore, a massive potential for Christians to make a difference in their neighbourhoods. That potential is being realized in the way a thousand flowers bloom in the villages, towns and cities of our land every day. What intrigues me is how little these connections are recognized in our teaching and in the conscious discipleship of most Christians. Sunday church and Monday's decisions are too often kept in isolation, not by design but by the accident and neglect of our church life and teaching. And maybe by the faint embarrassment many Christians have with a faith that's too overt. Someone said that most British Christians go to church as they go to the bathroom – with the minimum of fuss and with no explanation if they can help it.

The other deficit in our whole-life discipleship is the difficulty we have in relating our faith to the major social and political issues of the day. At the local and personal level, Christians are often deeply involved in acts of kindness and commitment, but the biggest question of our time has a global reference. Put simply: 'How then shall we live?' Given the bewildering complexity of an interconnected, online world with its huge potential for technological advance or disaster, in a planet that's rapidly becoming exhausted and where we never seem able to stop fighting – how then shall we live together in a finite and fragile space?

Christians believe the answer lies in a radically different world view, one that honours God as Creator and Jesus as the trailblazer of a new path for humanity. We need to stop playing religious games and start seriously following Jesus. Eugene Peterson calls discipleship 'long obedience in the same direction'.[7] Extreme discipleship will involve everything we've got, what Jesus called loving God 'with all your heart, and with all your soul, and with all your mind and with all your strength' (Mark 12.30). It will involve constantly turning our lives towards God as a sunflower constantly turns its face to the sun. It will involve having the love of God and the life of Jesus as our constant points of reference. It will involve living in God's world, in God's way, with God's help.

That's what it means to be a disciple.

They said this

A man can no more possess a private religion than he can have a private sun or moon. (G. K. Chesterton)[8]

Do all the good you can, by all the means you can, in all the ways you can, in all the places you can, at all the times you can, to all the people you can, as long as ever you can. (John Wesley)

When Bob Geldof met Mother Teresa he was both impressed and daunted by her work. 'I could never do what you do,' he said. She held his hand and said, 'Remember this. I can do something you can't do and you can do something I can't do. But we both have to do it.' (Alan Hargrave)[9]

Taking it further

Anchor passage: Romans 12.1–2, 11–end
Read once, take a full two minutes to reflect, then read it again.

To think about

Opener: 'Present your bodies as a living sacrifice . . .' How healthy do you think your body/whole self is as a disciple of Christ? What would a 'spiritual doctor' say?

- Where are we, and most Christians, 'conformed' rather than 'transformed' (v. 2)?
- Which of those short, sharp exhortations in vv. 11–21 do you find most of a challenge?
- When do you think you have received most help from your church in living out your faith from Monday to Saturday?
- What would you like your church to do to help people relate their faith to the everyday decisions that face them?
- What area of your discipleship would you most like to get sorted out?

Prayer: Write on a small piece of paper an area of life that you intend to integrate more fully with your faith this week. Pray over it quietly, offering it bit by bit to God. Then place the piece of paper in a wallet or handbag, and resolve to look at it again at the end of the week to see what you and God have done about it.

Gracious God,
you make all ordinary things to be holy,
and all holy things to be of use in the world.
Help us to see all of life as a gift
and our whole life as an opportunity to serve and to save
through the love you pour into our wounded world.
We ask this through Jesus Christ our servant King.

PART 1

Facing God

———•◦•———

Until I was 31 I was confident I could achieve more or less any task I took on in ministry as long as I had enough time to do it. After the age of 31 I knew I needed God's grace and strength to do anything at all. What made the difference was an episode of nervous exhaustion, when I found that all the essential organs of my body were making their displeasure known at the same time because they were being starved of sufficient energy to perform their normal tasks. I needed to stop. From then on I knew from experience rather than from theory that I needed the strength and wisdom of God to be an effective disciple.

What's the problem?

Former Archbishop William Temple once wrote: 'When we fail in discipleship it is always for one of two reasons: either we are not trying to be loyal, or else we are trying in our own strength.'[1] If we are to be followers of Jesus it's important that we follow and don't try to get in front of him. It's possible to believe we believe in God when in reality we are only believing in ourselves and our own capacity to be Christians.

In running the Christian race it would be a strange disciple who ran with a full-length mirror held out in front of him, enabling him to look at himself, assess his own performance and adjust his own appearance for maximum effect. And yet that's what it can seem like if we make our point of reference our own selves, so that it's 'my faith', 'my ministry', 'my spirituality' and so on that absorb us. 'How am I doing?' may be a legitimate question every so often, but Christian living is not an exercise in narcissism. Our constant point of reference as disciples has to be the figure of Jesus.

How could we think about this?

I remember a conversation I had with an ordained RE teacher when I had recently found a faith for myself rather than a faith from my family. I was trying to explain the difference I now experienced, and spoke about now being a 'committed Christian'. He rather abruptly asked me what I meant by a 'committed Christian' as opposed to an ordinary one. I was irritated; it was so obvious. Once it had been a faith in which I believed in God in an unexamined and ineffective way and went along to church in pursuit of girlfriends; now it was a faith with the living Jesus Christ at its heart and the promise of a deepening trust and friendship with God for a lifetime.

I might have been a little gauche in the way I expressed myself but there is, surely, a difference in those two versions of Christian faith. Even if we have been lifelong, faithful members of the church community, most of us can identify a time when faith became a more significant dimension of our lives, when the graph of faith went up more sharply. Christians have all sorts of ways of describing the experience: 'God moved from the edge of my vision to the centre', 'a second-hand faith became a first-hand faith', 'God moved from optional to essential in my life', 'Jesus stepped out of the pages of the Gospels and into my own experience.' In my case I often say that I had many of the pieces of the Christian jigsaw scattered around, but I seemed to have missed the big central piece – the living Jesus – and it was when that piece went in that the rest of the jigsaw fitted into place.

This move from the edge to the centre is when the journey of discipleship properly starts. Before that, the Christian faith is rather like looking at maps and reading guidebooks; after that, faith is walking the paths among the lakes and mountains, and following the Guide who knows the territory like the back of his hand.

The move from one to the other, however, has no blueprint. After all, we may cross a border into a new country by simply wandering along a country path with minimal awareness of where we're going, or by coming to a border post and making a conscious decision to enter the new territory, or by rushing through a highly defended border-crossing with guns blazing around us. Whichever way it is, we find ourselves in new terrain and gradually, over time, the differences in the countryside, the architecture, the language, the culture, become clearer. The culture of the kingdom of God should emerge naturally as one of love, justice and joy as we travel deeper into its heartland.

The journey of faith, therefore, may be quick or slow, or quick–quick–slow. It may be alone or accompanied, more intellectual or more emotional in character, and with a wholehearted or a fingertip faith as a result. No matter how it happens, what matters is that the journey has entered a new and potentially exciting phase, and the term 'disciple' seems appropriate at last. It's sobering to remember that Jesus never seems to have invited anyone to come to church (synagogue). It isn't churchgoing that is of the essence of being a Christian, but following Jesus on the path of daily discipleship, being different and making a difference as we go.

☆ *In 1938 . . . I [Simone Weil] was suffering from splitting headaches; each sound hurt me like a blow . . . I discovered the poem . . . called 'Love' [by George Herbert]. I learned it by heart. Often, at the culminating point of a violent headache, I make myself say it over, concentrating all my attention upon it and clinging with all my soul to the tenderness it enshrines. I used to think I was merely reciting it as a beautiful poem, but without my knowing it the recitation had the virtue of a prayer. It was during one of these recitations that . . . Christ himself came down and took possession of me. In my arguments about the insolubility of the problem of God I had never foreseen the possibility of that, of a real contact, person to person, here below, between a human being and God.* (Simone Weil)[2]

Disciples may be said to enter a pattern of relationships (a dance), which in the Christian faith is called the Trinity – God as Father, Son and Holy Spirit. You can't take a dance apart without losing its beauty, so it's undoubtedly artificial to analyse the dance of love in the Trinity too much. Nevertheless, when disciples participate in the life of the Trinity, it means being:

Fascinated by God The God question haunts our society but to Christians it has the added quality of a holy fascination. This is a God who cannot be smaller than infinity, even though sceptics insist on trying to lay God out on a table as one object in a field of objects. The only concept of God worthy of the name is one who 'imagined' the universe into being and sustains it by his thought. This is no divine errand-boy waiting to do trivial tasks for us. This is the God beyond creation who nevertheless invites creation to join the dance of love for love's sake. I gladly admit to being fascinated by God, and happily have my vision of God enlarged by scientists, enriched by artists, and deepened by theologians. There's enough material to explore here for an infinite number of lifetimes.

Friends of Jesus Christ This is the term used by Jesus in John's Gospel when he reminded his disciples at the last meal they had together that he didn't call them servants but friends (John 15.14, 15). We inherit that privilege. Christ invites us into that intimacy which St Paul consistently describes as being 'in Christ' – although he also describes the relationship as: knowing Christ (Philippians 3.10), receiving Christ (Revelation 3.20), Christ living in the believer (Galatians 2.20), and more. 'Friendship' is another lovely metaphor. As present-day followers of Jesus Christ we're just as much like Keystone Cops as the first disciples, running around without much clue as to what we should be doing, but we might get a little less erratic if we keep our eyes on this best of all friends.

Full of the Spirit A prayer often on my lips at the start of the day is that I may be full of the Spirit so that I can live in God's world with God's help. The problem is that we all leak. The image of a football in the corner of my study tells the same story. Because it has a puncture it's partially deflated and therefore whenever it's kicked its shape is distorted: if it were punted down the field it would sink to the ground without a bounce. If the puncture were to be repaired, however, and new air blown into it, the football would resist the kicks and be full of bounce. It would be what it's meant to be. In the same way, Christians, full of the Spirit, would become the followers Christ invites them to be. Of course, this is the ideal; we are all punctured to some degree or other, but 'fresh air' is always available.

What could we do differently?

This section of the book is probably the shortest but it's the most important. We can't live this Christian life in our own strength. It's too demanding, too much of a foreign language in our society, to tackle by ourselves. All the rest of the book depends on getting this first stage in our discipleship right. We need to face God and draw on God's limitless life.

The characteristic stance of disciples, therefore, is that they have their lives turned towards God as their consistent point of reference. This is as practical as it is profound. At any time through the day the disciple is able to remember the presence of God, without needing to be unduly pious or to show off by random levitation. Looking in the direction of God for a moment is a timely action whenever we do it. It puts things in perspective, it reminds us whose we are and whom we serve, and it opens us to grace. But even more than this intentional looking towards God, having our lives turned in his direction is an attitude of life and a disposition of the heart. The ideal is that it's 'just the way we are', whatever we're doing.

To help us live our lives facing God we have the gifts of Scripture, sacrament, prayer and the fellowship of the Church. These are the four legs of a sturdy table where we can sit and eat. We ignore this feast at our peril because this relationship with God is like any relationship – it doesn't flourish on nice thoughts and good intentions; it needs time, love and commitment. Discipleship starts with a life that characteristically faces God, and loves to do so. We live in the gaze of God, and one way of describing the life of discipleship is that we spend our lives trying to return that gaze. To be held in that gaze, and to return it forever, is to be in heaven.

From that vantage point all of life takes on a different meaning. Every action is significant as one that may reflect the invigorating presence of God. George Herbert caught this precisely in the words of a well-known hymn:

> Teach me, my God and King,
> in all things thee to see;
> and what I do in anything
> to do it as for thee.
>
> A man that looks on glass,
> on it may stay his eye;
> or, if he pleaseth, through it pass,
> and then the heav'n espy.
>
> All may of thee partake;
> nothing can be so mean
> which, with this tincture, 'For thy sake',
> will not grow bright and clean.
>
> A servant with this clause
> makes drudgery divine;
> who sweeps a room, as for thy laws,
> makes that and the action fine.
>
> This is the famous stone
> that turneth all to gold;
> for that which God doth touch and own
> cannot for less be told.

If we look through the surface level (the glass) of any action we can see deeper significance (heav'n), and by doing it 'for thy sake' even menial tasks (sweeping a room) can take on meaning ('makes that and the action fine'). This is the secret of discipleship (the famous stone). Any part of our lives, offered to God, can be turned to gold.

They said this

The one thing truly worthwhile is becoming God's friend.

(Gregory of Nyssa, AD 395; the last words of his last book)

If you can stand where Jesus is standing, you can say what Jesus says; you can come to God as father without going through a lot of complex religious or ritual conditions. To be with him is to be – so to speak – under a clear sky, with no intermediaries between you and the maker of all things . . . He has marked out the place for us all to stand. (Rowan Williams)[3]

God is like love going everywhere.

(Amanda, age five, apropos of nothing at all, striking up another theological conversation at the tea table)

Taking it further

Anchor passage: 2 Corinthians 5.16–end
Read once, take a full two minutes to reflect, then read it again.

To think about
Opener: Share the most interesting experience you've had this last week as you've tried to be a disciple of Christ – an encounter, an activity, a conversation, something read, something prayed, something understood.

- Everybody looks up to, or follows, someone. Who or what do people we know love to follow?

- Share the most significant phase of the journey you took in coming to your own faith.
- In what ways do you think you are different now from the way you would be without faith? (Or is 2 Corinthians 5.17 not true?)
- How do you try to live with your life 'turned towards God'?
- What verses or phrases of the anchor passage stood out for you as spot on, or as needing further exploration?

Prayer: The group pairs off and each person is asked to turn and look fully into the face of the other. (If you are alone, use a mirror.) This might cause embarrassment, but that's part of the point. It's hard to look with a steady, searching and caring gaze at another person who isn't your life partner. Continue to explore the other's face, what you see, what you wonder at and wonder about. Then turn back and pray silently for that person, holding them before God who sees us fully and loves us. The leader draws the prayer time together.

PART 2

Facing myself

———◆◆◆———

After facing God, the greatest mystery I ever have to explore is myself. Each one of us is a complex web of origins and motivations, devices and desires, but it's only as we grapple with practical issues such as money, sexuality and healthy living that we come to understand this mysterious 'inscape'. The test of character, as of faith, is practical. And through this fascinating territory we look to God to guide us as we try to live gracefully and well. Living faithfully starts very close to home.

1

Living gracefully

———•◆•———

The story is told of writer Graham Greene waking up in the middle of the night convinced he had just got hold of the most seminal literary plot in the world. He wrote it down on a pad by his bed so he wouldn't forget it and then went back to sleep. In the morning he woke and reached eagerly for the pad to see what this wonderful idea was. It said: 'Boy meets girl. Boy loses girl. Boy gets girl back.'

The most significant ideas are often the simplest. One of the simplest and most basic of all Christian beliefs is that God loves us, actively and unconditionally. It's so obvious we often forget to say it. God's love isn't qualified by how worthy we are to receive it. Nor is it doled out grudgingly by a curmudgeonly God. Nor is there a finite quantity of love that God has to give, so more for one means less for another. God's love is limitless and given with an outrageous profligacy. Christians call this 'grace'.

What's the problem?

Strangely, although we talk about grace a lot, many Christians find it hard to accept God's grace for themselves. As well as whatever deprivation of affection we might have experienced as a baby, this is probably due in part to our awareness of our own failures and a stubborn belief that we have to earn the approval of significant others. We think God knows what we're like inside and, with that knowledge, can't possibly love us without turning up his nose at least a bit. If God really is going to love us, he must surely put a few conditions on that love. You can't just give love to an unrepentant loser without some kind of accountability. After all, that's what we ask if we're giving our money to a charity – we need to know it will be well spent and not wasted. Surely God's grace must have some kind of tariff?

I once preached a sermon that involved wandering down the aisle and giving a £10 note to a young man who, not unnaturally, looked somewhat bemused at this unexpected gift. I told him I didn't want it back and gradually he began to grasp that it really was a gift and he didn't have to earn it in any way, nor would I ask anything of him in return. But it was hard for him to accept and for others to accept too (Why him? Why not me? and Why do I feel like that?). Accepting a gospel of grace is a major challenge to a culture that values everything in terms of financial exchange.

But if we get stuck in this kind of spiritual accountancy we're likely to find ourselves caught in a web of legalism. The life of faith becomes an exercise in the avoidance of judgement, and trying to earn points in the divine ledger. Many people think of the Christian faith as a way of rules, regulations and restrictions. They see people who adhere to a faith as controlled by an outworn morality and somehow diminished as human beings, and the awkward truth is that some Christians do indeed choose their certainties, construct their fortresses and defend them against all comers. The generosity, freedom, love and forgiveness of the gospel seems to have been consigned to the cellar, like a boisterous dog, and only allowed upstairs if absolutely necessary. And yet grace is an irreducible 'given' in the Christian life because it's the very nature of God.

And what we have received, we need to give. To have been embraced and liberated by grace is the platform from which we can then try to live gracefully with others.

How could we think about this?

With Jesus it's always 'yes'. He met every problem and every temptation by saying 'yes' to a more vivid alternative. Would people say that of us?

Look at the early chapters of John's Gospel. In chapter 2 Jesus is producing fine wine by the bucket. In chapter 4 he's multiplying loaves and fishes like a bakery. In chapter 6 he's talking about living water that pours out forever. All these images are of superabundance, of outrageous grace. Is that our faith?

Jesus faced legalism many times in the Gospels and he doesn't seem to have budged an inch. Grace is free – full stop. Look at the story of the workers in the vineyard who started work in the last hour of the day but received the same pay as those who had laboured and sweated throughout the day. When the latter group complained at the injustice, Jesus told them, in effect, that in an economy of grace, generosity, not merit, is the key. Everything is levelled up, not levelled down (Matthew 20.1–16).

Look at Jesus on the cross and remember the words of the famous hymn: 'Were the whole realm of nature mine, that were an offering far too small. Love so amazing, so divine, demands my soul, my life, my all.' It's one of the most humbling hymns I ever sing and easily brings tears to my eyes. There's no limit to what we are given or what is asked of us.

The advice of one bishop to his clergy was to be 'generally mad and prayerful in the world'. That's a liberating challenge, and very different from carefully picking our way through a minefield of moral certainties and restrictions on our lifestyle. Augustine's advice was to 'love God and do as you like'. If we are anchored in God we are free indeed.

☆ *A white soldier and a black woman confronted each other at the South African Truth and Reconciliation Commission. The soldier had taken away and killed her son. Later he had taken away and killed her husband. When he asked her for forgiveness she replied: 'You are asking for amnesty. I am asking for three things. You dragged my son out of bed and took him away and killed him. I want to be taken to the place where his body is buried so that I can pay my respects to him. You took away my husband and I never saw him again. I want* to be taken to the place where he was shot, so that I can see where it happened and pay my respects. You have taken away my whole family and I have no one to give my love to, so I want you to become my son, and come and drink tea with me once a week.' And he did.

What could we do differently?

- Stay close to the grace-giver. Ask yourself who, among all the people who have passed through your life, has been a truly graceful person. There will be many you have liked and loved, but who would you say was full of grace? The people I have known like that have had deeply attractive personalities. Essentially they have been Christlike, and that's the ultimate goal of any Christian life. It's a strange conviction for which I can offer no adequate substantiation, but it seems to me that long-married couples often end up resembling each other (or their dog). If we stay close to Christ daily we might end up a bit like him.
- The most difficult place to live gracefully is with our immediate family and close friends. This is where irritating habits build up into iconic moral failures and where resentments reach epic proportions with potential criminal consequences. This is truly the acid test of grace and sadly many of us fail it; statistically Christian marriages fail as often as those of no faith. Living gracefully here requires three senses: a sense of proportion (is this really a global disaster?); a sense of humour (a smile and a shrug is easier than three hours of painful silence); and a sense of humility (could it be that *just occasionally* I may *almost* have done something *very mildly* irritating as well?). Look at the life of Jesus and you don't see him snapping back when others are being obnoxious, except where the poor are being oppressed. In the ministry of Jesus you see grace embodied. Stay close to that man.
- Forgiving another person is a hard-fought gift. It's not always possible and should never be demanded of someone else. In many cases it's a journey; someone might be able to forgive one day and not the

next. And yet the alternative may be vengeance or sullen resentment. A Chinese proverb says: 'Whoever opts for revenge should dig two graves.' But when a victim is able to forgive a perpetrator we witness a miracle and a supreme act of grace. And annoyingly, the forgiveness comes first. It doesn't wait and see if the other person apologizes: it acts as though the relationship has already been made good, even before that has happened. That's why it's a miracle. Remember too that on the cross it wasn't actually Jesus who forgave his killers; he asked his Father to forgive them. That can be a life-saver to those who find they can't do it themselves.

- Start each day with a clear intention to be full of grace and generosity. Imagine your life full of the Spirit. It's a prayerful discipline to ask for that grace and believe that it's given. We know that grace will get used up during the day. I can lie in a warm bed in the morning and think how I'll live gracefully all through the day. I'll spread God's love to everyone I meet. Today I'll be a saint. Then I get out of bed and meet real people! We start out full of desire to be graceful, but so easily we become disgraced. But that's OK. There are tiny shoots of green grace growing in the back garden of our lives, and some of them are getting quite strong. Quietly, the Gardener is at work in us.

They said this

We are here in church because we don't deserve to be. [It's all grace.] And when that truth gets hold of you and sinks down inside you like a hot drink on a cold day, then the effect on the whole life of the Christian community is quite marvellous. We are all here by grace alone, so we can relax. You don't have anything to prove in the presence of God. (Tom Wright)[1]

God sent into the world a unique person – neither a philosopher nor a general, important though they are, but a Saviour, with the power to forgive. Forgiveness lies at the heart of the Christian faith. It can heal broken families, it can restore friendships and it can reconcile divided communities. It is in forgiveness that we feel the power of God's love. (Queen Elizabeth II)[2]

People are unreasonable, illogical and self-centred. Forgive them anyway.

If you are kind, people may accuse you of selfish ulterior motives. Be kind anyway.

If you are successful, you will win some false friends and some true enemies. Succeed anyway.

If you are honest and frank, people may cheat you. Be honest and frank anyway.

What you spend years building, someone may destroy overnight. Build anyway.

If you find serenity and happiness, they may be jealous. Be happy anyway.

The good you do today people may forget tomorrow. Do good anyway.

Give the world the best you've got anyway.

You see, in the final analysis, it's between you and God; it was never between you and them anyway. (Mother Teresa of Calcutta)

Taking it further

Anchor passage: Ephesians 2.1–10
Read once, take a full two minutes to reflect, then read it again.

To think about
Opener: When, and from whom, have you known completely unconditional love? What was it like? What effect did it have on you?

- In what ways has your experience of faith been similar to, or different from, that human experience of unconditional love?
- What does it mean to be 'saved' (v. 8)?

- Has your experience of forgiving others been a struggle, a journey, a decision, or what? What would you say to the priest whose daughter was killed in the 7/7 London bombings and who declared she could not forgive with integrity?
- What verses or phrases of the Bible passage stood out for you as spot on or as needing further exploration?
- Paul emphasizes God's initiative (grace) in vv. 4, 5, 7, 8, etc. He also says that, previously, we 'were dead through [our] trespasses and sins'. How would we explain those concepts to someone exploring faith?

Prayer: Hold a coin in your hand. Imagine that the face on it is someone you find it hard to be graceful towards. Pray for that person and your relationship with them as you hold the coin carefully and firmly, in silence. Then place the coin under a central lighted candle or other symbol and read the passage from Ephesians again.

2

Knowing God's guidance

————◆•◆•◆————

The apocryphal story is told of a young missionary who was always looking for clear divine guidance. He said he had gone to work in South America because when he was seeking guidance he had suddenly seen a bar of chocolate with Brazil nuts in it. He was therefore clear that God was guiding him to Brazil. His sceptical friend asked: 'What would you have done if it had been a Mars bar?'

This only serves to remind us that guidance is an area of Christian discipleship ripe for silliness. More importantly it's an area of considerable confusion and needs addressing with a clear head as well as an open heart.

What's the problem?

It's strange how God always seems to guide us to do what we want to do. This should immediately raise our suspicions. Moreover, a small alarm bell always starts ringing in me when someone says: 'God has told me to do so and so.' The problem is so often that God hasn't told the rest of us the same thing. There's ample scope here for self-deception and manipulation.

The way that some Christians look for God's guidance suggests a kind of code-breaker mentality, as if God loves setting cosmic codes or a series of puzzles for us to solve. What picture of God lies behind such an understanding of God's interaction with his creation, I wonder? It would be a strange parent who left a series of clues for a child to work through in order to learn where breakfast had been hidden.

Underlying this image may be an uneasy concern about why God doesn't make his guidance any clearer for us to understand. If God loves us as he is supposed to, surely he would let us know what's best for us with much greater clarity. This corrosive doubt can begin to wear away at our belief in the trustworthiness of God. Prayer is an essential part of finding our way ahead, but God isn't hiding some vital clue until we crack the code.

The code-breaking approach to guidance reinforces a tendency in some Christians to over-spiritualize Christian living and decision-making. They seem to float a few feet above reality and it makes believers seem faintly ridiculous. A bishop wrote to a vicar to offer him a new post. The vicar replied that he must go away and pray about it. The vicar's wife went upstairs to pack. (Both are necessary.)

How could we think about this?

First, it's important to be clear that God is not being deliberately obstructive. The biblical witness is that God is always wanting to communicate his love for us. His is a way of opening up and liberating people from being in thrall either to magic or to the oppressive control of others. Jesus always brought light and hope to people as he widened his hearers' horizons and set heaven before them. God doesn't play games with us.

It follows from having this confidence that it would be very strange if there were only one course for our life, and that if we missed it by making a wrong choice at some apparently innocent juncture we would irretrievably be on plan B. It's much more in keeping with a God who opens up possibilities that he is with us at every juncture of our journey, helping us to make *our* decisions, and then working with us to make the most of the choice we've made. This is how he takes us seriously as adults who have to take responsibility for our own lives and decisions, but in the good company of the God who wants only the best for us, and who doesn't control the world through robotic formulas. God has a *vision* for us, more than a *plan*. Plans expect no real variation, while visions allow many routes to their fulfilment. God's vision is that we should 'come to ... the knowledge of the Son of God, to maturity, to the measure of the full stature of Christ' (Ephesians 4.13). There are many ways to achieve that exalted life, and none of us is discounted if we make mistakes or follow false leads along the way. Thank goodness.

Following that through, it's obvious that God is giving us free will in a free world. God's interaction with his world is much better seen as undertaken from the inside rather than the outside – he 'under-rules' rather than 'over-rules'. The alternative would be a God who swamped the world with his will and gave no opportunity for those values to flourish that give life meaning – love, compassion, courage, trust, the pursuit of justice, peace and truth. What would be the point of a world where God guided his people with words of flame in the sky or voices in the kitchen? We would have no option but to submit and obey, but not through love. A God who works through relationship and with the fuel of love is always going to be much more interactive in his dealings with us. We journey together in friendship. God is always both *at* our side and *on* our side.

Interestingly, the Bible never talks about 'guidance' but it does give us plenty of evidence of a Guide. The Old Testament is full of people interacting with God for good or ill, and Jesus lived his entire life based on his intimacy with his Father. If you are driving in heavy traffic in a strange city and get lost, you might stop and ask a local how to get to your destination, but the danger is that you would get a set of complicated instructions that you couldn't possibly remember. Much more helpful would be if the pedestrian offered to get into the car himself, saying: 'I'm going that way too. Can I come with you and we'll find the way together?' Not guidance but a Guide.

☆ *A man was wandering through the heat of the desert. He seemed to be looking for something. His name was Macarius and he would become one of the founding saints of the Egyptian Coptic Church. His problem was that he knew God was calling him to build a monastery, but he didn't know where. He searched the wilderness, asking God to show him the right place to build it. 'Please show me,' he prayed. 'Give me a sign.' But God was silent. At last, after another fruitless day, an angel appeared with a message from God: 'The Lord is not going to show you where to build the monastery. He wants you to choose the place. If he tells you where to build and things go wrong, you will only blame him. So you must choose.'*

What could we do differently?

- We need to open our minds and not half-close them. If I need to wear glasses it would be very strange if, when I put my glasses on, I then closed my eyes, relying on the glasses to do the seeing for me. Glasses are not a substitute for using my sight but an aid in doing so. Because of them I see more clearly. Thus, seeking God's guidance is not an alternative to thinking hard and responsibly for oneself but an aid to that process. Prayer enables us to think and see more clearly, and hopefully come to the conviction that some course of action is the best way forward.
- It's important when we try to make good decisions, and to involve God in the process, that we use a multifaceted approach. The wisdom that comes from the regular reading of the Bible and a disciplined life of prayer is paramount. This gives us hope that we are being shaped into having what Paul calls 'the mind of Christ' (1 Corinthians 2.16). To try and 'read off' the meaning of a random verse of Scripture as applying directly to our own situation is a strategy fraught with danger, although God is not proud and sometimes does seem to give us that connection. I've known Christians who've said they've opened the Bible randomly and found a verse that has been exactly right for their decision, and who am I to complain? (Though the danger of turning up 'He went and hanged himself' – Matthew 27.5 – and following it with 'Go and do likewise' – Luke 10.37 – is a well-known warning!)
- Other levels of discernment can and should be added to these fundamental gifts of Scripture and prayer. Conversations with wise friends (and we usually know who those should be) can lead us to look with a more level eye, and perhaps to emerge from the fevered indecisions of our own minds. There's a lot to be said for sanctified common sense

coming from good Christian friends. The way circumstances work out, and the doors that open and close, are also part of the decision-making process. In the end we're listening for the 'loud thoughts' of our own hearts, inspired by God. This is where the decision has to be made.

- Someone I knew had resisted a call to ordination for years. It constantly nagged away at her but she pushed it away with many good, practical answers. In bed one Sunday morning she felt sure she was going to receive a clear sign that day, one way or the other. She was relieved when no one arrived to take the crèche that morning, so she hurried into that role, feeling safe. However, on the loudspeaker relay from the church, she heard the person leading the service say: 'Someone here today is trying to decide about ordination. Know that God is calling you.' She had cancer and thought that was another good excuse, but then the nurse at the cancer centre, who knew nothing of the turmoil in her mind, said to her: 'I don't know why, but I keep on seeing a picture of you with a dog collar on.' She gave in and became a fine priest – before the cancer claimed her and her ministry was fulfilled in the nearer presence of Christ. Here was a person shaped by Scripture and prayer, who was open to what circumstances and other people said, and finally listened to the loud thoughts in her own heart, all under the loving eye of God.

- We might note, finally, that one of the important things to do in seeking to make a good decision with God's help is to get on the move and not be paralysed by self-absorption. You can only guide a car when it's moving, and God can often only help us when we're taking responsible decisions and maybe even moving in one of the possible directions before us. Only then might God be able to redirect us. There's an old fable of a donkey that had two piles of hay to eat from, but died because it couldn't decide which one to choose. Get moving.

They said this

Gideon laid a fleece before the Lord to test a decision (Judges 6.36-40). But it is important to note that the fleece was laid after the decision had been made – it was not a way of shirking responsibility. Requests for signs should be confirmatory rather than predictive and need only be made in special cases. (Ken Costa)[1]

If only God would give me some clear sign. Like making a large deposit in my name at a Swiss bank. (Woody Allen)[2]

Taking it further

Anchor passage: Psalm 139.1–18
Read once, take a full two minutes to reflect, then read it again.

To think about

Opener: Have you had an experience of what you would regard as God's good, clear guidance?

- This passage emphasizes God's profound knowledge of us rather than his guiding of us. How does this very comprehensive knowledge help us in this question of guidance?
- 'In your book were written all the days that were formed for me, when none of them as yet existed' (v. 16). Do you think God knows everything that is going to happen to us?
- 'God has told me to do so and so.' How would you respond when someone says that?
- 'God has a vision for us more than a plan.' Do you agree with that, and if so what are the implications?

Prayer: Identify someone you know who is confused about the best way ahead in some area of his or her life. With your hands on your knees, hold that person in the palm of your hands, as a picture of what God does, and pray for a clear sense of direction. If you can, make contact with this person during the week and be a listening ear as he or she discerns the way forward.

3

Handling money

---•◆•---

In March 2012 an executive director of a major investment bank resigned, saying that 'after nearly 12 years at the firm the environment now is as toxic and destructive as I have ever seen it'. His resignation letter went on:

> It makes me ill how callously people talk about ripping their clients off. Over the last 12 months I have seen five different managing directors refer to their own clients as muppets . . . I hope this can be a wake-up call to the board of directors [to] weed out the morally bankrupt people, no matter how much money they make for the firm.[1]

Money has a terrible power to corrupt. Even if we have little of it we easily fall for the devil's lie that a little bit more will sort out our life. If money is the measure of all things then it slips into the driving seat of our life and soon starts to break the speed limit. And yet money is morally neutral, neither the be-all and end-all, nor something to be rejected as 'filthy lucre'. It's what keeps food on our plate and a roof over our head. In any case, as Woody Allen said: 'Money is better than poverty, if only for financial reasons.' How can we forge a healthy relationship with money?

What's the problem?

Greed Let's not put too fine a point on it. There's a deep sickness in the heart of humanity, across every race and culture, which obsesses about accumulating more and more money, and will use moral short-cuts and justifications of every kind in order to do so. When wealth becomes our goal it becomes our god and everything then serves that false divinity. Somehow we seem to think that more money will bring us happiness, but the evidence is that it's like drinking salt water: it just makes us more thirsty. We also run the risk of cutting ourselves off from others. Brazilian bishop Dom Helder Camara said: 'Money has a dangerous way of putting scales on one's eyes, a dangerous way of freezing one's hands, eyes, lips and heart.'

Corruption One of the great sadnesses of human nature is that it's terribly open to corruption. It's one of the tragic convictions of our time that 'everyone has their price'. Westerners are appalled at the corruption that siphons off foreign aid and investment to provide luxuries beyond imagining for the elite in developing countries, but fail to notice the tax evasion and avoidance that's taken for granted as 'fair game' at home. Between £80 billion and £120 billion in tax goes unpaid in the UK every year – at least £25 billion is unpaid, £35 billion is illegally evaded and £35 billion is avoided by legal but arguably immoral means.[2] Jesus warned about the way we notice the speck in someone else's eye and not the log in our own (Matthew 7.5).

Inequality The pay gap between the highest and lowest earners in society is widening all the time. The average top to bottom pay ratio in FTSE 100 companies in the UK in 2010 was 262:1. The estimated average total pay for a CEO in a FTSE 100 bank was £6.4 million, 565 times the National Minimum Wage, and this at a time when banks have been bailed out by the state and are still performing poorly.[3] No amount of protest seems to get through the armour plating of corporate self-interest.

Giving Christians are good at giving – but not *very* good. People of faith generally give more money to charity than others but the biblical goal of giving a tithe (10 per cent, however that 10 per cent is calculated) is mysteriously elusive. It's very hard for us to free ourselves from the seduction of personal ownership whereby we are convinced that everything we have is ours, but which brings us into stark conflict with the biblical view of wealth, to which we now turn.

How could we think about this?

The most important starting point is the conviction of David that: 'All things come from you and of your own have we given you' (1 Chronicles 29.14). David had assembled all that was needed for his son Solomon to build the Temple, but rather than get smug about all this wealth he reminds his hearers that we always stand in a chain of life and material possession. Everything has its origin before we appear on the scene, and the ultimate Originator is God. 'All things come from you.' This means that anything we have we have on loan. It's very hard to break open the fantasy of ownership; I fall into it all the time. Perhaps we should start each day with this verse from 1 Chronicles. Everything comes from God – our life, our health, our very breath; the ability to walk to the bathroom, to have food on the table for breakfast, to have a car on the drive; to see the sun through the trees and smell the freshly cut grass. It's all a gift, not a possession. Money, like life, is on loan.

Then we need to remember the negative side of this. Paul was adamant: 'The love of money is a root of all kinds of evil' (1 Timothy 6.10). Not money in itself but the love of money in a way that elevates it above its role as a means of exchange. There's nothing inherently dirty about money. It enables society to function and confers great blessings on us all. God doesn't want us all to be poor and miserable. However, we can't ignore the rough ride the rich receive from Jesus in the Gospels. It's not because they are rich; it's because their wealth has inoculated them against noticing the poor, and no one is truly rich while others are truly poor.

One of the loveliest assertions of the New Testament in relation to wealth is Paul's conviction that 'He will always make you rich enough to be generous' (2 Corinthians 9.11, Good News Bible). This may look counter-intuitive to someone struggling to make ends meet, but seems to be borne out by experience time and again. If we give first, there's always enough; if we give last, there isn't. Moreover, Paul says: 'Each of you must give as you have made up your mind, not reluctantly or under compulsion, for God loves a cheerful giver' (2 Corinthians 9.7). We have used that last phrase more easily than we have believed it. Cheerful giving, joyful, energetic, liberating giving, is still a goal for most of us, but those who practise giving *from the heart* constantly report how easy it is. As someone said: 'You can't take it with you so why not send it on ahead.'

Money is a good servant but a disastrous master. Kept in its place, wealth is as good a way as we've got of keeping the world moving economically, but when it assumes a life of its own – as when the banks were creating impossibly complicated financial products before the credit crunch – it becomes a monster. 'Where your treasure is, there your heart will be also' (Matthew 6.21), and it will rule your world. Perhaps we need to learn individually the deep, hard lesson that our whole world order is having to face, that growth in itself is not a believable goal. Our economy is predicated on growth, but Tim Jackson, Professor of Sustainable Development at the University of Surrey, says bluntly: 'The idea of a non-growing economy may be an anathema to an economist. But the idea of a continually growing economy is an anathema to an ecologist.' For lasting prosperity he proposes looking outside the conventional trappings of affluence to relationships, family, community and the meaning of our lives and vocations in a society that values the future.[4] Christians will recognize those criteria. Enough is enough; we need to consume less 'stuff'. Relationships matter more.

☆ *A strong man in a circus once tossed up an orange with his left hand, caught it in his right hand and with one motion squeezed the juice from the orange so that there couldn't be another drop remaining in the mass of pulp. He then challenged anyone in the audience to come forward and extract another drop of juice. There was silence, and then a small, pale-looking man stepped down into the ring. He took the orange, squeezed the pulp, and finally produced three more drops of juice. The strong man was amazed and asked him how he did it. 'Easy,' said the little man, 'I've been a church treasurer for the last 30 years.'*

What could we do differently?

- We could be more thoughtful about balancing our expenditure. Why do we think we need this item? Could we borrow it or put off that purchase a bit longer? Are we considering buying that new car or flat-screen TV because we feel somewhat ashamed of our old one? What's that feeling of shame all about? Do I need those books that I don't stand a chance of reading until retirement? Do we eat out and over-spend rather more often than we need? And what does our pattern of spending say to our children and grandchildren? Having money to spend is a privilege and responsibility in a world where 1.4 billion people live on less than £1 a day. It's not something to spend without due care and attention. Let's examine how we use our money.

- We could say grace more often! We may say grace before meals, but we might also say thank you before entering a food store, going to a concert, reading a book, going for a walk – because we're fortunate to be able to buy food, have access to great music, know how to read and have the health to walk. If everything we have is on loan to us or sheer gift, it's good to remind ourselves of our dependence on the grace and goodness of God and the world that God has filled so magnificently.

- We could pay taxes gladly, without grudging and sniffing disdainfully. The New York heiress Leona Helmsley is quoted as saying: 'Only the little people pay taxes,'[5] but if that's the case then the little people are the honourable ones. Governments have the responsibility of turning money into real human value as they provide basic requirements for those who need them – which means all of us. If we have a high income we should be proud that we can pay high taxes (how counter-cultural is that?).

- We could give as a joy and not as a duty. This is the plain teaching of 2 Corinthians 9.7. Giving should also be:
  - ➢ *prayerful* – an act of thanksgiving as we give ourselves 'first to the Lord' (8.5);
  - ➢ *planned* – but not prescriptive (8.10, 11);
  - ➢ *proportionate* – realistic to our income (8.12);
  - ➢ *a priority* – first not last (8.3).

We might tithe, using the Old Testament measure of one-tenth of total income to church and charity. Or we might give an hour's pay (or more), having calculated our total income and divided it by the number of hours we normally work. Or we might give out of sheer generosity because of our love for Jesus who 'though he was rich, yet for your sakes he became poor, so that by his poverty you might become rich' (2 Corinthians 8.9). A wise old clergyman once said: 'Think of the figure you want to give – and then double it!'

- If we are genuinely short of money it's good to remember than God loves a cheerful *receiver* as well as a cheerful giver. Don't let's be afraid of receiving the generosity of others – that, after all, is the whole basis of a gospel of grace with a God who acted first and fully in Jesus Christ, without receiving anything from us to earn such love.

Christian jargon about money

'The Lord is blessing us' (meaning: we have lots of money).
'We're wondering what the Lord is saying' (meaning: we're only just paying our way).
'Perhaps the Lord has completed his work' (meaning: we've run out of money).

They said this

When a small number of people try to appropriate for themselves the things that belong to all, quarrels and wars break out, as

though nature were indignant at the sight of the cold words
'yours' and 'mine' which introduce division where God has set
unity. These words are empty of meaning; they express no reality.
You are stewards of the goods of the poor, even when you have
acquired them through honest labour or by inheritance. The
greatest harm that you suffer from being rich is that it takes
you away from the happy slavery of Jesus Christ.

(St John Chrysostom, *c.* 347–407)

It begins to seem like there's nothing money can't buy. Except of
course the things that really matter. There's nothing wrong with
being rich so long as we remember that. Money can't buy eternal life.
Money can't buy the forgiveness of sins. Money can't buy the faith
that moves mountains. Money can't buy the love that will not let
us go. These are things that everyone can have but no one can buy.

(Sam Wells)[6]

Taking it further

Anchor passage: 2 Corinthians 8.1–15
Read once, take a full two minutes to reflect, then read it again.

To think about
Opener: How difficult are we going to find it in a moment to talk about
money and giving? How can we talk honestly but without embarrassing
anyone?

- 'Their abundant joy and their extreme poverty have overflowed
  in a wealth of generosity on their part' (v. 2). Can you explain that?
  Have you experienced it?
- Read vv. 7 and 8. Do you see this as manipulation and how do you
  feel about Paul writing in this way?
- Why are British Christians, by and large and in contrast with
  Americans, so coy about money and so reserved in their giving?

- 'It is a question of a fair balance' (v. 13). What is a fair balance when the church roof needs repairing but many churches in Africa don't have a roof?
- How could your church renew its understanding of money and giving?

Prayer: Imagine you have £100,000 to give away. In silence, think how you would divide it, and why. After a few minutes' thought (and jotting down if necessary), share what you would do with the money. Then pray for those people and organizations who would receive your gifts.

4

Handling our sexuality

———◆◆◆———

I have a cartoon of Adam talking earnestly to Eve in the Garden. Eve
looks a little nonplussed. The caption says: 'Adam tells Eve he'd like to
start dating other women.' It's a good job we can laugh about sex because
it keeps sex in perspective. The problem is that sex is so powerful it's like
electricity – it can electrocute and destroy us, or it can light up our lives.

I remember reading in one of our popular newspapers that the
average male thinks about sex every eight and a half minutes. I always
wonder who takes the trouble to find out this kind of information and
how they do it, but I have to trust my red-top informant! I also once
noticed the TV listings for BBC2 read like this:

9.40 *Adult Lives* First of ten films examining contemporary British
views of sexuality, starting with a Christian couple
who refuse to have sex or live together until they are married.
[Clearly this is aberrant behaviour.]
10.00 *Adult Lives* Profile of Jenny, a dominatrix prostitute.
10.30 *Newsnight*
11.30 *Adult Lives* Homosexual rituals of courtship.

Every angle on sex is constantly explored for an expectant, fascinated
public. We live in a society saturated with sex, and Christians are part
of that society. How can we live wisely and well with our sexuality and
the sexual obsession of contemporary society?

What's the problem?

It's obvious that sex sells. Alluring female forms are attached to every conceivable product in the advertising firmament, from cars and cameras to cardigans and kitchens. Unfortunately, these female forms are so far beyond the reach of most women as to induce feelings of envy or failure or even self-disgust. Still more unfortunately, we have seen the growing phenomenon of the sexualization of childhood as manufacturers have realized the massive commercial potential of children who want to keep up with their friends or grow up fast. The consumerization of society is almost complete, and sex is the key. Moreover, erotic material has moved from top shelf to mainstream. E. L. James' *Fifty Shades of Grey* sold over five million copies in six months.

Allied to this sexual takeover is the emotional separation of sex from relationship. As one famous actress said of an affair: 'Although horizontally everything was lovely, vertically we didn't get along.' And a 17-year-old girl lamented in an article in the *Sunday Times*:

> It's all casual sex now; nobody talks about love. I wish I could have a real connection with a man. But there's no courtship any more. That's all dead. It's just immediate. You're expected just to look someone up and down and make the decision just like that: are you going to have sex or not?[1]

Sex is being reduced to functionality and athleticism.

We haven't found an effective way of helping single Christian people to inhabit their sexuality. We have simply said that sex is only for married couples and the alternatives are either celibacy or life in a monastery or convent. As our sexuality is an integral part of our identity, this has been rather less than helpful. Given the pressure in society to prove our value by our sexuality and for the young to prove their acceptability by their sexual prowess, this can produce an intolerable tension for those single people who don't want to play by those immature rules.

The Church has another particular problem area – its inability to handle issues related to gay sex. The battle rages worldwide over the question of the equal validity of lesbian, gay and heterosexual relationships. The Anglican Church especially has been deeply troubled, split as it is between those who hold to an apparent biblical aversion to gay sex and those who see the biblical witness as being more nuanced. More heat is being generated than light, and in the meantime much of society looks on with scathing disbelief.

How could we think about this?

The most important initial stance for Christians to take is to be positive about sex as God-given and great. See the Song of Songs for details. Christianity is an embodied faith. It celebrates a God who was so 'down to earth' that he incarnated his own life in the life of a human being. This is a God who 'saw everything that he had made, and indeed, it was very good' (Genesis 1.31). All matter matters in a material world. Sex is a brilliant part of that world, giving joy, delight, playfulness, forgiveness and wonder to human relationships and the necessary process of peopling the world with the next generation. But sex is so sensational it needs to be handled with care.

Christians will want to maintain stubbornly that sex is relational and mustn't be reduced to the functional release of sexual energy (although masturbation is a different case unless it's relationally destructive). The tender bonding of two people operates at a psychosomatic level in which emotional, intellectual, spiritual and physical elements are ideally kept in balance. Sex intensifies as the whole relationship intensifies. As confidence in the permanence of the relationship grows, so too would the physical intimacy. Of course, the balance will never be entirely even, as different dimensions of the relationship take centre stage, but the isolation of the physical as the measure of intimacy can cause real damage to the human psyche and to the capacity to sustain mature relationships thereafter. In the UK, 30 per cent of young men and 26 per cent of young women have had their first experience of sex by the age of 16,[2] and as long ago as the year 2000 it was being reported that only 1 per cent of men and women aged 16–24 have their first experience of sex in marriage.[3] Given these social realities, it's all the more important that Christians speak realistically about the holistic nature of human relationships and of having the sexual element kept in balance with the development of the whole relationship, without being prescriptive on how that holistic approach works out for individual couples.

For a Christian, sex is ultimately sacramental in that it's 'an outward and visible sign of an inward and spiritual grace'.[4] It energizes and sustains the intimacy of the couple in lifelong, faithful commitment to each other. The idea of sex as sacramental is so far removed from society's way of thinking that it needs serious reflection among Christians as to how we live with that disjuncture. The sadness of so much contemporary sexual activity isn't that too much is given but that not enough is given. Christians put the highest value on sex, but they see it as a glorious gift and not as a cheap souvenir.

However, if we are thinking honestly about sex it has to be admitted that it can make fools of us all, and especially Christians who think they are secure in their moral castle. The record of clergy adultery isn't anything to be proud of. Close fellowship and a compassionate nature can leave Christians vulnerable to an eruption of passion that takes their breath away and leaves them scrambling for a reason why their situation is different from others'. 'So if you think you are standing, watch out that you do not fall' (1 Corinthians 10.12).

It's important that lesbian and gay sex isn't an obsession for Christians. We need a sense of proportion. There are seven verses on the subject of homosexuality in the entire Bible, compared, for example, with hundreds on the subject of poverty and the oppression of the poor. On the one hand, some Christians consider the issue is crucial because it relates to Christian anthropology and the whole way we understand the nature of humankind. On the other hand, many Christians think the biblical references are to exploitative, promiscuous sex, not the faithful, permanent relationships gay Christians may aspire to. The upshot is that the issue has to remain in the liquid solution of the Spirit and not be allowed to become hardened and encrusted. Christians can differ in their understanding on issues that are not essential to the truth of the gospel. The essential thing is not to allow the issue to become an obsession and a litmus test for Christian orthodoxy, and to ensure that churches fully welcome everyone, whatever their sexuality.

What could we do differently?

- It's important that Christians are positive about sex as a joyful part of being fully human and fully alive. We could examine our instincts to make sure that we are not always negative about sex (as society thinks we are) and not looking for ways of criticizing others. It leaves the impression that Christians are secretly jealous that other people are enjoying more sex than they are. And we do have a bit of history to live down – Augustine called women 'a temple built over a sewer', and Origen had himself castrated!

- It's also important not to be simplistic in thinking about sex, imagining that we have all the answers because we know our Bibles. The whole arena of sexuality is more complex psychologically, biologically and spiritually than most of us imagine. None of us should condemn another, except when abuse is involved. The latter of course requires the full engagement of the law and of therapeutic intervention. For the most part, however, Christians need to think intelligently about these issues by reading, hard thinking and honest discussion.

- Christians seem to have a black-and-white approach to sex. If you are married then all is well; if not then sex is taboo. A healthier approach would be to recognize a spectrum of sexual needs and expressions. At one end would be the faithfully committed and loving married couple, while at the other would be the irresponsible, predatory and promiscuous young person. But in between are all sorts of other situations – an engaged couple living together, a single person unsure of her attractiveness, a special friendship that has an element of physicality, a widow who longs for human touch again, a married man who has a fling and feels guilty, a married woman who has a long-term lover, a man without affection at home who sometimes goes to prostitutes . . . The range on the spectrum is vast and the stock Christian approach looks decidedly blunt. When the religious elite were condemning the woman caught in adultery, Jesus bent down and drew in the sand, embarrassed at their hypocrisy. His approach to the woman was much more sensitive, understanding and honest (John 8.1–11). That needs to be our model.

- Furthermore, we could all do with self-examination before God on matters sexual. How well integrated are we in our thinking, our fantasies and our attitudes? Men in particular sometimes avoid such dark areas through jokes and self-justification. The tiger of sexuality prowls around in the basement, and if we keep it locked away down there it may escape one day and wreak havoc around the house. Equally, if we overindulge it as a house-guest it might do the same and claim we gave it permission! The crucial truth to hold on to is that even if we can't help our instincts, *we can help what we do with them*. Indulge sexual fantasy and it will flourish in the warm glow of our affirmation. Better to thank the fantasy for its visit (it shows we're still alive sexually) but usher it out of the back door. The house belongs to God (1 Corinthians 6.19).
- The fact that society is obsessed with sex doesn't mean that we all have to be. We have a number of key questions to keep before us:
  - ➢ Who is my neighbour? (Is my attitude to her or him healthy and for that person's good?)
  - ➢ Who is my God? (Who rules my world?)
  - ➢ Who am I? (A slave to my instincts or a pilgrim trying to learn a better way?)

They said this

Love is the answer, but while you're waiting for the answer, sex raises some pretty good questions. (Woody Allen)

The idea of celibacy before marriage is meaningless if it is enforced by a jealous god; it is a beautiful idea but it is made beautiful by personal decisions rather than authoritarian edict. If young people do not grasp 'the idea' we must not blame them or accuse them of lust and abandon. It is the failure of the church to interest them in the idea that sex without love robs them of their dignity, they become meat and no more. We have failed to explain that sex is sensational which is why it is so precious.   (Peter Owen Jones)[5]

The reproduction of mankind [*sic*] is a great marvel and mystery. Had God consulted me in the matter, I should have advised him to continue the generation of the species by fashioning them of clay ...   (Martin Luther)[6]

Taking it further

Anchor passage: 1 Corinthians 6.12–20
Read once, take a full two minutes to reflect, then read it again.

To think about
Opener: Think back over the week. What evidence did you see of the preoccupation of society with sex? Consider news stories, adverts, TV and films, conversations, books, magazines, consumer goods, the internet and so on.

- 'I will not be dominated by anything' (v. 12). In our sexualized culture, is that easier said than done?
- 'Whoever is united to a prostitute [and, by extension, to anyone who is not a spouse or serious partner] becomes one body with her. For it is said "The two shall be one flesh"' (v. 16). Is that truth still relevant to people, now that so many have sexual relationships of a more 'recreational' kind?
- Is it your experience that Christians are no different, or considerably different, from others in society in their sexual attitudes and behaviour? And if the latter, how do you think they do it?

- How do you think church teaching, either locally or nationally, should be brought to bear on our sexual obsessions and confusions? Is there teaching we ought to nuance, and how do we engage honestly with issues that are so sensitive?
- What do you think is the way through our dilemma on gay relationships?

Prayer: Lay out some night lights in a circle around a cross, or make a cross shape with the night lights. Invite members of the group to think of people whose lives are in confusion because of sexual issues and then to light the candles silently, praying for those people as they do so. Then take a few minutes of silence to reflect on our own sexual history and attitudes, praying in gratitude and in confession.

5

Facing temptation

The writer Hilaire Belloc said: 'Don't worry about avoiding temptation; as you grow older it starts avoiding you.' It's tempting to believe that. Certainly some temptations melt away along with the disappearance of the waist, but others are lifelong. We learn to recognize the shadowy wolves tracking us through the forest, ready to pounce. We know the familiar routines and negotiations. We have our strategic plans and our tactical failures. But whether the temptations are to do with drink, sex, gambling, spending money, lying, overeating or a hundred other obsessions, the problem is compounded by the truth that Franklin P. Jones identifies: 'What makes resisting temptation difficult for many people is that they don't want to discourage it completely.' I'm afraid so. And none of us is exempt.

What's the problem?

After a while of facing temptations and losing time after time, the next move is to fall into disabling guilt. Guilt hangs around us with varying degrees of weight, which we sometimes experience almost physically lying across our shoulders. And it paralyses us. We find ourselves in a familiar, smooth, high-sided chute, propelled into unwelcome repetitions and unable to summon the energy or imagination to do anything different. Temptation becomes obsession, and the question the Christian asks (dimly, because not able to stop the slide) is the

48

fundamental question of discipleship: 'Who or what is my God in this place?' Is it the God and Father of our Lord Jesus Christ, or is it in practice my particular obsession? Who's in charge?

The scale and impact of society's obsessions is alarming. Even calling them 'society's obsessions' is disingenuous: these are *our* obsessions, the responsibility of individual persons, families and human groups. However, the impact of these issues is certainly experienced at a societal as well as a personal level.

- *Alcohol* The Office of National Statistics in 2011 reported that 33 per cent of men and 16 per cent of women in the UK were 'hazardous drinkers'. In fewer than 20 years the number of alcohol-related deaths in the UK has doubled to nearly 9,000. (In the United States it's said to be 100,000.) Of UK household expenditure, £40 billion goes on alcohol. Alcohol consumption per head has doubled in the last 50 years.[1]
- *Pornography* There are 420 million internet porn pages, 4.2 million porn websites and 68 million search engine requests for porn every day.[2] One in three ten-year-olds have seen pornography online and 81 per cent of young people aged 14–16 regularly access explicit photos online, with 12- to 17-year-olds the largest group of internet pornography consumers.[3] This suggests that their earliest introductions to sex give them no norm against which to compare these images of sexuality. An American study also found that 56 per cent of divorce cases involve one party who has an obsessive interest in pornographic websites.[4]
- *Drugs* There has been some success in tackling drug misuse. Nevertheless, drug use among 16- to 24-year-olds in 2009–10 was 20 per cent, and the figure reported by 11- to 15-year-olds was 22 per cent. Over 5,000 hospital admissions in the UK have a primary diagnosis of a drug-related mental health disorder.[5]
- *Gambling* The Gambling Commission in 2010 reported that there are over 450,000 'problem gamblers' in the UK. The gross gambling yield, after winnings have been paid, was £5.6 billion.[6]

These sample statistics mean that there are a lot of troubled people and chaotic families trying to survive in a society that constantly reinforces messages of success, achievement and happiness. The reality for many families, including Christian families, is that life is an unending battle with dark forces and salvation does not feel near at hand.

How could we think about this?

There's no blame attached to facing temptation. It's what we do with it that matters. Paul is reassuring:

> No testing has overtaken you that is not common to everyone. God is faithful, and he will not let you be tempted beyond your strength, but with the testing he will also provide you with the way out so that you may be able to endure it.   (1 Corinthians 10.13)

Even so, in practice the promise is easier to claim than to experience. God is certainly faithful and will never leave us, but 'the way out' may be a profound struggle. It may be some comfort that we are not alone and that our temptations are 'common to everyone'. There's a worldwide fellowship of strugglers.

It's important not to be too 'spiritual' about dealing with temptation. Those who call us to higher spiritual planes, exhorting us to sail above the things of the world and to claim the victory, may leave us with a persistent desire to punch them on the nose. There's many a battle going on in Christian hearts and homes. General Gordon of Khartoum used to call his main temptation Agag, after the Amalekite king. He often wrote in his diary: 'I had a hard half hour this morning hacking Agag in pieces before the Lord.' We need to be honest, because over-spiritualizing the battle with temptation can often increase the isolation and guilt.

It can also be an error to isolate the temptation as if it's an entirely renegade part of our life. This can lead to an unhealthy 'splitting' of our personality into good and bad, and lead also to destructive self-hatred.

Jesus told his disciples they were to love their enemies (Matthew 5.44) and to love their neighbours 'as themselves' (Matthew 19.19). He knew that the best way to overcome your enemy is to make him or her your friend, and the best way to deal with persistent temptation may not be to disown it but to bring it in from the cold, to understand its roots and offer it a healthy place in our lives rather than an unhealthy corner. The temptation to drink too much may be due to a more fundamental problem of stress that, when addressed, may allow alcohol a more civilized place in our life. An obsession with sex may be saying something about unsatisfactory human relationships that need attention.

☆ *Two monks came to a river where there was a young woman unable to cross because of the strong current. One of the monks offered to carry her across on his back, which he duly did. The two monks set off again in silence. After a few miles the other monk said to his companion: 'Doesn't it worry you that you carried that young woman across the river when we're not supposed to have any physical contact with women?' 'Ah,' said the other monk, 'I put her down five miles ago; I think it's you who are carrying her now.'*

The temptations of Jesus give us plenty of material for thinking about our own problems. They've been categorized in many ways by preachers searching for a shape for their sermon. For example, they can be seen as the temptation to be relevant (turning stones into bread), to perform (throwing himself off the Temple) and to be powerful (by worshipping the devil). The interesting thing is the way Jesus responds to each of the temptations by calling the devil to a deeper allegiance. He turns the focus away from his own dilemma and back to God – we live by the words that come from the mouth of God; God is not to be put to the test; God alone is the one to worship. The problem with temptation is that it often operates at the level of trivia and there are more serious issues of life, peace, justice and integrity that need to be addressed. With everyone he encounters, Jesus deepens the conversation.

The 'dark grace' of temptation subverts our cocky self-sufficiency and should turn us to a deeper dependence on God. When we know our own finitude and helplessness we will usually more easily look to the One who promises to travel every dangerous path with us and hold us firm. In time, as we grow in confidence, we might find new strategies and strengths from our divine Friend and Tutor.

Jesus also set before all those he met a more vivid alternative in how to live. He always resisted negativity for its own sake. He saw the hundreds of fine wires that enmesh and constrict us and longed to cut through them and release us into a fuller way of living. That's the way to face temptation – there's something so much better that we are made for.

What could we do differently?

- The 12-step programme of Alcoholics Anonymous (AA) is a well-trodden route through the minefield of temptation and addiction. Of the original 12 steps, half include direct reference to God or 'a Power greater than ourselves'. There is a profound recognition that 'this kind can come out only through prayer' (Mark 9.29) – and hard work. The American Psychological Association summarized the process as follows:
  - ➢ admitting that one cannot control one's addiction or compulsion;
  - ➢ recognizing a higher power that can give strength;
  - ➢ examining past errors with the help of a sponsor;
  - ➢ making amends for these errors;
  - ➢ learning to lead a new life with a new code of behaviour;
  - ➢ helping others who suffer from the same addictions or compulsions.[7]
- Crucially, in AA they do this together. The support of the AA group is central. Here is the honesty, comradeship, understanding and mutual strengthening that each person needs. I once knew a senior priest who said his AA group gave him more fellowship than any church

group he had ever known. What applies to alcohol applies equally to any other addiction or obsession, and where an actual group doesn't exist, perhaps an online group does. But the 12-step programme isn't a panacea. It's reported that of those who start attending a group, only 19 per cent are there after 30 days and only 5 per cent after a year.[8]

- If at all possible, finding one non-judgemental person to talk to is a true gift from God. People experience much shame over these issues and many Christians find it hard to open themselves to someone else, but a spiritual companion offers safety, an outlet, wisdom and implicit forgiveness. However, the trust we give to such a person is enormous and the decision about who is able to hold that trust must be made very carefully.

- Voluntary, personal boundaries are important tools for self-management or recovery in the field of temptations and addictions. For example, with alcohol a boundary could range from a complete ban for a recovering alcoholic to weekends only for someone aware of his or her potential fragility, or the three-day-a-week recovery period recommended by doctors. Someone tempted by internet pornography would probably have to put him or herself under an absolute ban because of the insidious nature of the obsession. So too with online gambling. Fail-safe mechanisms of personal control may have to be devised.

- The really difficult balance to find is that between having clear boundaries that we're determined to keep, and not beating ourselves up if we don't succeed. If we're not determined enough then we're already permitting and planning our downfall, but if we're too rigid with ourselves we set up cumulative guilt and the danger of 'splitting' and self-hatred. Finding the balance is an art, not a science, but art fully informed by self-awareness and a generous understanding of human nature. Above all, perhaps, we need to commit to *a direction of travel* and not to immediate success. The Prodigal Son was still on his way when the Father saw him and ran to meet him. He hadn't yet arrived.

- One of the best ways of dealing with temptation is simply to get a life! There are many alternative interests and hobbies that could give a constructive outlet to obsessive energies. The full tapestry of opportunities for most people is remarkably rich; we just don't see them. Finding a clear direction, purpose or commitment is a game-changer for many, and finding faith is the ultimate game-changer for some. When someone is mired in a personal struggle with a particularly deep-rooted compulsion, it may be hard to remember that Jesus came promising abundant life, and he hasn't changed the offer. And part of that abundance is simply 'fun'. We disciples are encouraged to enjoy ourselves because we enjoy God, the giver of life. If we have fun we weaken the grip of other compulsions.

They said this

'All things are lawful for me', but not all things are beneficial. 'All things are lawful for me', but I will not be dominated by anything . . . You were bought with a price; therefore glorify God with your body.

(St Paul, 1 Corinthians 6.12, 20)

Some junior devils were trying to tempt a holy hermit, without success. Their master came along and told them that wasn't how it was done. 'Watch carefully,' he said. He then approached the holy man from behind and whispered in his ear: 'Your brother has just been appointed Bishop of Alexandria.' Immediately a scowl of furious jealousy crossed the hermit's face. '*That's* how it's done,' said the devil. (Folk tale)

Taking it further

Anchor passage: 1 Corinthians 10.12–13
Read once, take a full two minutes to reflect, then read it again.

To think about
Opener: Without giving away any confidences, has your experience been that many Christians are facing these same struggles and often failing?

- 'If you think that you are standing, watch out that you do not fall' (v. 12). What do you think and feel when a Christian leader falls from grace, and what do you think might be the best way to respond?
- 'He will not let you be tested beyond your strength' (v. 13). Do you think that can be guaranteed?
- How do we find the balance between having clear boundaries and high standards for our own behaviour and being gentle with ourselves when we (inevitably) fail? Do we tend to be too tough on ourselves or too gentle?
- Does our church get the balance right? And what about the national Church?
- If we are all 'walking wounded', how can we be more open with, and supportive of, each other?

Prayer: Give each person a piece of A4 paper and then ask them to screw it up, thinking of anyone they know whose life is 'screwed up'. Then hold the screwed-up paper gently in cupped hands and pray for that person and all the others who are affected by his or her dilemma. Then gently smooth out the paper and place the pieces before a cross. Finish with prayer.

6

Being healthy

———•◦•◦•———

I once lived for five days on £1 a day for all my food and drink. This was like surviving all week on two Starbucks coffees. My wife and I carefully worked out quantities of lentils, where to get the cheapest tin of mushy peas, and how much a tea bag cost. The low point came when I was hosting a dinner at an Oxford college and, among the wonderful food and fine wines, I was eating dhal and drinking water. The point of the exercise was that 1.4 billion people on our planet are living on less than £1 a day for all their needs – food, shelter, education, healthcare and so on. And not just for five days but every day.[1] The long-term effect on me has been to make me realize that food and health are not only political issues, they're also emotional, spiritual and theological issues. Issues of discipleship.

What's the problem?

Globally, there's a tragic inequality in diet. Every so often this inconvenient truth moves across our television screens as a particularly outrageous famine strikes some part of Africa, but the perennial reality is probably too shocking for us to contemplate. Half the world is overfed and half the world is underfed. The same link between poor diet and poor health is seen to some extent in our own country. You see it in the streets. Social disadvantage leads to poorer health and lower life expectancy. Within a mile of where I live, life expectancy is ten years shorter than it is for me.

In the West we've developed a dangerous obsession with body image. There's massive media coverage of the perfect body, reinforced constantly by advertising, glossy magazines, TV and films. The ideal of slim and shapely women and good-looking, muscular men is blasted at us from all sides, and young people in particular are acutely vulnerable to such pressure. The result can be low self-esteem, social isolation, catastrophic diets, anorexia and permanent physical and psychological damage. In teenagers, the issue of body image and the subsequent distress over how they see themselves is extremely serious, undermining confidence, leading to self-rejection, illness and self-harm. Studies show that 80 per cent of women are dissatisfied with their bodies (and just for the record, I'm not too happy with the way I look, either . . .).[2]

Our unbalanced approach to our health is made worse by living in a 'fix-it' culture where we expect experts to be able to manage and cure our problems through medical technology. The medicalization of life has been parodied as 'I will lift up my eyes to the pills . . .' Pills, operations and other medical interventions are supposed to sort out our difficulties – 'Why else do we pay our taxes?' we ask. A moment's thought, of course, makes us realize that health is a multi-layered phenomenon requiring the co-operation of the individual, the family, social attitudes, health professionals, politicians and more; but the expectation nevertheless remains that 'they' will have an answer, and we're entitled to it.

How could we think about this?

If we are trying to live faithfully, our starting point will be to remember that every human being is made in the image of God and reflects God's glory. That in itself is a huge contrast to the reductionist, mechanistic readings of human life prevalent in much contemporary thinking. Christians share the delight of Ferdinand as he looks at Miranda in *The Tempest* and exclaims: 'O you wonder!' There is a wondrous quality in every human being simply because we are made in the image and likeness of God. Nor are we just spirits trapped in a disposable body. We *are* our bodies, energized by mind and soaked in spirit. And this precious reality has been valued fully and finally in God choosing to re-enter his creation in a human life and body, that of Jesus. If we wanted a vote of confidence in the value of our bodiliness, we couldn't do any better than that. Building on that affirmation, Paul can later declare that we are nothing less than temples of the Holy Spirit (1 Corinthians 6.19). These bodies we have and are can be seen, in a sense, as divine reproductions – even though that may not be our first thought when standing naked before a full-length mirror.

Health was a major preoccupation of Jesus' ministry. He restored people to health at every turn; indeed, this characteristic ministry almost overwhelmed him and he sometimes had to slip away to maintain his own health and sanity. When he sent his followers out on their first mission he told them to 'preach and heal' – these were to be the core tasks of his disciples (Luke 9.2). Jesus was concerned for people's total health, which meant the integration of physical, psychological and spiritual well-being within a social context of justice and freedom. This is why mission and medicine have always gone together in Christian history. The story of Christian mission is inevitably the story of healthcare and education. It's still the case that 40 per cent of primary healthcare in sub-Saharan Africa is supplied by the churches.[3]

Perhaps the most beneficial way to start thinking about health is to make friends with our bodies. Whatever its shape and vulnerability, this body is me, and it's miraculous. It's so miraculous, in fact, that it deserves the very best care and attention I can give it. Abusing my body is therefore deeply saddening, as well as dangerous. Cancer Research UK says that 100,000 people die from smoking-related diseases every year, which is like losing a city the size of Exeter or Blackburn every 12 months.[4] Our bodies deserve better than that. My body is an honoured part of God's world and I need to live comfortably and appreciatively with it.

A doctor said 'I've been practising medicine for 30 years and I've prescribed many things. In the long run I've learnt that for most of what ails human beings, the best medicine is love.' 'What if that doesn't work?' he was asked. 'Double the dose,' he replied.

What could we do differently?

- It follows that a first way of addressing our ambiguous relationship with our own health is to take responsibility for our bodies and their well-being. This involves eating and exercise. I need to tread carefully here, lest derisive cries come from my family. However, without it becoming an obsession, our diet needs careful attention to keep it healthy, balanced and moderate. This usually means avoiding the latest fads and sticking to common-sense reductions and balances. The weight-loss industry often only bears witness to its own narcissism and to our insatiable desire to look good. It's the deeper commitments that matter, and as well as our own food intake we need to care about that of the next generation. Obesity is a medical time-bomb in the West.
- One practical way of ensuring that eating is seen as a responsible exercise (and pleasure) is to say grace more often at main meals. Eating is a spiritual issue, and to say thank you is to respond to a God whose generosity is abundantly evident. A meal is then not just a fuel-stop but an occasion to make a contribution to both health and fellowship. Saying grace doesn't need to be a desperately pious activity. One of our graces is simply: '(*Leader*) We should be grateful. (*Response*) And we are.'
- The issue of exercise is equally tricky. Persuading those who need exercise to go to the gym is only slightly more difficult than keeping up that membership after the first few weeks. At its simplest, three half-hour episodes of good cardio-vascular activity a week (like swift walking or swimming) will do immense good. Olympic success ought to spur many of us to roll off the sofa a bit more often. But still the seduction of computer, phone and games technology keeps millions

of young people stranded before a screen. (Writing this makes me determined to try again and get out there . . .)

- We could take an intelligent interest in the NHS. This means moving beyond slogans, and evaluating and caring for an institution of which the rest of the world is envious. It's the best part of the post-war welfare state and mustn't be taken for granted. One of my daughters and I sometimes sit on opposite sides of the River Thames, she in her senior post in Guy's and St Thomas' Hospital and me in the chamber of the House of Lords. Both of us care deeply about the NHS, flowing like a deep, strong river between us. Both politicians and practitioners on either side of the river take responsibility for this splendid institution, but those who use the river, who sail in it and navigate it as patients, should also take responsibility and engage in important debates. The NHS is too important to be left to any one group in society. How much do you and I know about how the NHS locally actually works?

- We could be more deeply committed to minimizing global inequality in health. In the United States there is one doctor for every 300 people, and in the United Kingdom one for every 416, whereas in Malawi and Tanzania there is one doctor for every 50,000 people. The Millennium Development Goals placed the reduction of child and maternal mortality as high priorities and good progress has been made. It's possible, but we have a long way to go. Sufficient food, clean water and basic medicines would make all the difference to a world sadly out of kilter with the mind and heart of its Maker. Our personal commitment to support aid agencies, fair trade, government aid programmes and those who are trying to make global trade relationships fairer, must surely be a central part of basic Christian discipleship. Hardly anything could be closer to the heart of Jesus.

- The role of prayer in personal health and recovery from illness is disputed territory, though one much subject to scientific study. The John Templeton Foundation is engaged in fascinating research on the relationship of spirituality and – variously – gratitude, forgiveness and happiness.[5] There seems to be a correlation between health and active spirituality, but it would be a mistake to push the link too far. What we can say from the personal testimony of countless believers is that people believe they experience genuine, profound benefit from their own prayer and the prayer of others. In whatever way we interpret this, it seems clear that prayer is good for you!

☆ *St Marylebone Church in London is home to a rounded health programme. From 1987 it has incorporated a Healing and Counselling Centre as well as an NHS Health Centre with a full range of standard medical practices and complementary therapies. St Marylebone Church has chaplaincies to local hospitals and clinics, and is the base for the ecumenical Guild of Health with its attempt to fuse together professional practice and spiritual resources. The church is also a centre for conferences and seminars on subjects related to health and healing, as well as offering the resources of the Christian healing tradition. Moreover, there are close links with the Royal Academy of Music, reminding people of the well-established links between music and a deeper understanding of what it is to be whole and to flourish.[6] This is holistic healthcare and a model for other parts of the Church.*

Taking it further

Anchor passage: Luke 8.40–56 (everyone should have their own copy of the text)
Explain that when the passage is read out everyone will be asked to identify one word or phrase that strikes them. Two minutes' silence will be given. These words or phrases are then shared, without any explanation. Then the passage will be read again and after a further two minutes' silence for reflection, everyone will be asked to say why they chose their phrase and what it means to them. Further discussion may follow. Having explained the process, try it out.

- What can we learn about Jesus and his way of healing from these two intertwined stories?
- The woman with the repeated haemorrhages was told her faith had made her well (v. 48). What can we say to faithful people whose prayers for healing aren't answered?
- Was Jairus' daughter dead? Does it matter? (Of course it did to her parents!)
- If overall we are becoming a healthier nation, what are the clouds on the horizon about which we should be concerned?
- How have we supported, or could we in future support, the NHS further?

Prayer: Who are the people on our hearts for whom we are praying or might pray at present? (Disguise the names if you fear they may not want to be known.) Share those situations. The leader writes the names down and then reads them out, giving ample time between each one for silent prayer. Each person pledges to pray every day for their person and to give a brief report on their situation at subsequent meetings. (The leader needs to make sure time is given for this at future group meetings.)

PART 3

Facing the world

———————◆◆◆◆◆———————

The call of God is to live faithfully in the particularities of daily life, not in a sheltered religious ghetto. This is where the hard work really begins. It often seems as if we have little clear guidance from Sunday about how to live on Monday. The questions become acute at our place of work, when we go shopping or when we're faced with the issues of peace and justice that bombard us in the news. There are two possible responses. Either we separate off our private religion from the rest of our lives, or we engage with the adventure of integrating our faith with the social, economic and political context in which we live. God's call is clear.

7

Working faithfully

———·•◆•·———

Living faithfully at work is a major challenge to most Christians. Of course I've only done a 'real job' for a very short time. I was a tram conductor for several seasons on the promenade in Blackpool (and have therefore seen the Illuminations more times than is good for anyone). So who am I to talk about work? It's both easier and more difficult to 'live faithfully' as a Christian minister. Easier because you are surrounded by the things of God all the time, and more difficult because you are surrounded by the things of God all the time. The bigger question for all of us is: 'What counts as work?'

When I'm at a party or on holiday or talking to someone on a train, I wait in hunted anticipation for the inevitable question: 'So what do you do?' I may obfuscate for a while but eventually it comes out and I wait while the other person readjusts her vision, checks back through her previous conversation for bad language, and plunges in again with the most innocuous statement she can think of at short notice. But I at least have a job. When a young mother who's staying at home is asked the same question she may feel a different kind of dismay. Does she say she's not working at present – in spite of the fact that she's working 18 hours a day on childcare – or does she says she's a teacher having a career break, or does she say she's a 'Chief Domestic Officer'?

What counts as work? What's work for, anyway? And how do we work faithfully, taking our faith to our work? How do we balance working life and the rest of life – and cope with stress and the spectre of unemployment and the bullying boss and the fear of failure? There are no 'click here' answers to all these questions, but let's examine the territory.

What's the problem?

Some people live for work while others hate it. Some are totally absorbed by their work, its structures and challenges, its rewards and relationships, while others see it as a necessary trudge to the weekend. What's a healthy Christian approach to work? Is it our primary route to fulfilment or an unwelcome invasion of our freedom? Is the world of work God-given or God-forsaken? I've exaggerated the two positions in order to clarify the problem. Most people are somewhere on the spectrum between the two poles, but the question lying innocently behind the difference is a basic one: what is work for?

Moreover, how can we avoid the consequence that for people at both extremes, and for many in between, work and home are completely different worlds? For Christians that usually means work is the God-free zone, with faith restricted to home and leisure, where God neither asks awkward questions about work nor offers powerful resources for it. The split is disastrous for anyone who maintains that the kingdom of God is all-inclusive and not just a hide-out for the religious. There are difficult ethical and relational issues in most workplaces, and these are God-shaped questions.

My experience of being wiped out by stress was enough to convince me of the reality of this all too common ailment. One in five visits to the doctor is because of stress-related illness. Should we just tough it out, recognizing that it's a fact of modern living, or is there a deep malaise in the workplace and in the pace and volume of our lives? We're tired of hearing about work–life balance, but is that because we've given up on it and are feeling guilty? On the other hand, there are very many people who would appreciate a bit of work pressure in their lives because they haven't got a job and can't see how to get a foot on the ladder. A million 16- to 24-year-olds in the UK have this different kind of stress.

A true story:

☆ *A student had a summer job in a factory that made jam rolls. All he had to do was send the roll through a machine and a man three metres away spread the jam on it. The student watched him. The man said nothing. After three days the man spoke. 'What do you do?' he asked. 'I'm at university.' 'What are you studying?' 'Politics, philosophy and economics.' The man thought for a moment. 'Blimey,' he said, 'that must be boring.'*

How could we think about this?

Work is part of God's original business plan. Work was part of his business in creation (not an easy start-up) and it was meant to be part of our business too, for we are created in the image of God. Work is part of our calling to be like our Creator and as such it's logically prior to what Christians call 'the Fall'. One writer notes: 'In the first chapters of Genesis God is seen to be a designer, builder, gardener, teacher, caretaker, legislator, social worker and tailor.'[1] We see God at work in the Garden, and our calling and privilege as God's image-bearers is to tuck in behind the divine purpose and to tend the Garden with him. The Garden is the precursor of the kingdom, the arena of God's goodness where his purposes are honoured and nurtured. This is where we can make a contribution, in tiny details every day, and it gives value to our work and our self-understanding.

We may note, however, that nowhere does God equate work with money. Work does not have to be paid to be significant. Work in the voluntary sector is just as valuable. Childcare is major work, for either parent. The equation of work with the earning of money is a hard one to break, however, and we may need to keep returning to the biblical picture of work as the expenditure of energy in the service of God and the world God loves.

The other side of work, of course, is that it's often a struggle. The story of the Fall reveals the truth that work isn't always a joy, that there's a gap between the ideal and the experience, that in a 'fallen world' the working environment is sometimes a battle zone. In this kind of world, so much has to be put right if the original 'business plan' is to be achieved. The eventual and conclusive answer to this search-and-rescue operation was the life, death and new life of Jesus Christ. The last words of Jesus on the cross as recorded by John are 'It is finished' (John 19.30), meaning 'It's accomplished' or 'Done it!' The work of God was completed, at incredible effort. But we are now enlisted in the ranks of those who have the cleaning-up operation to do after the great battle. That too is hard work, but what we do each day contributes to that task – or not. There are big issues at stake.

At the end of the 'great week' of creation God rested (Genesis 2.2). The idea of sabbath rest is a compelling vision carried right through the Bible, from creation to the Jewish law, from the rest the land needed in the seventh year to the ideal of Jubilee and the releasing of debt. The concept of sabbath had ossified by the time of Jesus and had often become a rigid restriction that Jesus was compelled to confront ('The sabbath was made for humankind, and not humankind for the sabbath'; Mark 2.27). Nevertheless, the essential insight is that we need a rhythm to our lives that creates space for re-creation, and this is a daily, weekly and annual balancing of our activities. Sabbath is a rich theme for exploration in a culture determinedly filling its time with more and more social, economic and emotional pressures.

Christians have sometimes struggled with the idea of ambition, seeing it as self-seeking and self-aggrandizing and in danger of making us tread on others. However, ambition can be redirected away from those destructive tendencies. We can be ambitious to be the best we can be, and to use our gifts in the most effective place. If ambition remains at the level of individual self-fulfilment it can be misused, but if it is seen in the context of God's vision for the whole human community – to which we contribute – then we have a healthy backdrop for our efforts to move on in our working life. I have always felt that I only wanted to be in the best place I could be to use whatever gifts I had, and I thought that was going to be in a parish because I had only ever wanted to be a vicar; but it still felt legitimate to accept the next challenge each time it came. The famous words of Olympic athlete and missionary Eric Liddell are relevant here: 'I know God made me for China, but he also made me fast, and when I run, I feel his pleasure.'[2] We want to feel God's pleasure in the work we do and it's right to attempt to get to that good place. But we won't feel God's pleasure if we've got there by ruthless self-promotion and stepping on others.

What could we do differently?

- If we are to integrate our faith with our working life (of whatever sort – paid, unpaid, voluntary, domestic), we'll need to recognize that God is already there in the workplace and asking us to live naturally as Christians, without denying our faith but also without excessive piety. A key verse to remember, and one with which I often start the day, is Colossians 3.17: 'Whatever you do, in word or deed, do everything in the name of the Lord Jesus, giving thanks to God the Father through him.' 'Do everything' means the way we do our work honestly, the way we relate to people with kindness, the way we look at moral issues responsibly. It means that we'll make decisions based on the widest view we can access, bearing in mind the human consequences. It means if people are having to lose their jobs we'll handle it humanely or protest honestly, and if there's a conflict to deal with we'll be reconcilers rather than aggressors. It means we'll encourage and be interested in the people around us and treat everyone with equal respect. Above all, we'll be remembering that Christ is there before us and asking us to work with him to redeem and enrich our working environment.
- If we're going to take the sabbath principle seriously we'll need to examine our diary carefully, and probably with the person we're closest to, in order to get some honest assessment of our self-justifications. There are many strategies to try – work no more than

two evenings a week, only work two out of three 'sessions' per day, protect Friday nights, have a family period each day, do no emails after eight, only turn on the smartphone every other day while on holiday. Everyone who tries to get their work–life balance right will have experimented with many ideas – and probably failed with several of them. In my own case I work hard between holidays but am generous with those precious times off. And I symbolically take my watch off at the start of the holiday! There are different stages of life and career to take into account as well, and different shapes to different jobs. So there are no rules except the main one – keep the sabbath, whatever it looks like.

- If we are under pressure that looks to be in danger of becoming stress, there are other strategies to try. The main one, of course, is to see a doctor, but the first step might be to examine the problem with a clear-thinking colleague, partner or friend and to break it down into its component parts. Like the proverbial problem of how to eat an elephant, it might then become possible to address the task bit by bit. Another ruse is to set aside a 'worry time' of, say, 9.00–9.15 each day, so that if you want to worry away at some problem that you don't want to invade the rest of your life, you refer the latest development, email, phone message or possible solution to that quarter of an hour the next day and refuse to tackle it earlier. Stress is insidious; we need to watch our inner emotional life for anxiety, and our outer behavioural life of sleep, eating, irritability and so on for warning signs – and give 'significant others' freedom to watch out too.

- Ministers of religion are often not best placed to help integrate work and faith outside their own vocational arena. The result is that people living busy and demanding working lives may feel they aren't understood or resourced by their church. Indeed, 50 per cent of Christians can't remember ever having heard a sermon on work.[3] What could churches do? A number have experimented with a slot called This Time Tomorrow (TTT) on Sunday morning, where a member of the congregation is interviewed about what he or she will be doing this time tomorrow: 'What kind of issues will you be facing?' 'What Christian resources would help you?' 'How could the rest of us pray for you?' It closes the gap between Sunday and Monday and helps everyone to realize we have an all-day, whole-life faith.

- Churches can also have members of the congregation preaching or being interviewed (at greater length than TTT allows) about being a Christian in their particular work setting. There can be generic or specialist house groups, or Sunday morning or weekday breakfast groups where work-related issues are discussed from a Christian perspective. I know one church that has Friday dinners for such conversations, and they've proved resoundingly popular. Intercessions in church can pray for 'white van man', council gardeners and supermarket staff as well as the usual doctors and teachers. The vicar could accompany a member of his or her congregation for a day at work to get a feel for the issues and complexities of being a Christian in that particular context. The possibilities are many, but first it's the mindset that needs a whole-life reorientation. As ever, change starts in the imagination.

They said this

Adam came out of Paradise with a wife and a spade.

(Bishop Ted Wickham)

A Christian secretary in an office may have the opportunity to 'pastor' more people in a day than a pastor; a doctor may have more opportunities to offer wisdom and comfort to those in suffering than a vicar; a 14-year-old at school may have more opportunities to share Jesus in a day than a paid youth evangelist.   (Mark Greene)[4]

When we declare truth even in small measure, the kingdom of God is advanced. This can be true when we draft documents, sell products, or mark exams – indeed, in any activity we do in our working day.   (Ken Costa)[5]

Taking it further

Anchor passage: Colossians 3.12–24 (or omit vv. 18–21 because it raises too many other issues!)
Read once, take a full two minutes for reflection, then read it again.

To think about

Opener: Where are the crunch points for you in relating your Sunday and Monday lives? Perhaps list on a flip chart.

- Vv. 12–16 focus on building up the inner life of faith. Do you find that inner life gets eroded through the week? What spiritual resources would help you integrate your faith with the rest of your life?
- How realistic is v. 17?
- Vv. 23–24 encourage wholeheartedness in our work 'as done for the Lord'. Are there jobs that cannot be done for the Lord? What would it mean for your work (paid, voluntary, domestic)?
- How could your church honour the world of work more effectively?
- Use George Herbert's hymn 'Teach me, my God and king' (see p. 14) as the basis of a verse-by-verse discussion on how it would work in practice.

Prayer: Share some of the deeper issues you're facing in your non-church life and work. Invite members of the group to jot down those issues so that they can pray for each other both now and in the coming weeks. Report back next time.

8

Going shopping

I admit it. I have a real issue with books, the problem being that I can't resist them. If I need a pick-me-up I buy a book. Indeed, I need only walk into a bookshop and I immediately see a paperback that plainly says 'pick me up'. No matter that I have, probably, hundreds of books at home that haven't yet been read but that I assure myself are just waiting for that long summer holiday. No matter that I have tried only to buy a book if I'm letting one go, or only buy a book if I have a book token. No matter that I tell myself the future lies with Kindle, I still buy books.

Many of us have obsessions like this in our shopping habits. TV mogul Simon Cowell apparently has 50 pairs of identical trousers in spite of it being a well-known fact that you can't wear more than one pair at a time. (He also has a Bugatti Veyron car that cost three-quarters of a million pounds.)[1] Shopping is the number one leisure activity for many people in the West today. To visit a shopping mall is to enter a consumer cathedral.

We have it all – but is that all we have?

What's the problem?

We all need to shop. The problem comes when shopping is an end in itself, when the point of the activity isn't the purchase of an object we need but the ritual of buying. Psychotherapist Susie Orbach wrote: 'Nothing would excite a young person more than the ability to buy, buy, buy and be famous. Contributing to society is not what it is about any more.

Image is everything.'[2] A young Chinese man reported in *Time* magazine said: 'My father's generation, they don't crave things like I do. His luxury is for the whole family to be together. People in my generation, we always want the next thing. It's how we express ourselves and live our dreams.'[3] Young people very often size each other up on the basis of what clothes and trainers they wear and what mobile phone they carry. This determines their social status and acceptability. Adults too scrutinize each other's clothes and accessories for subtle signs of their socio-economic status. We construct the identity we want to have (or are forced to have) by the purchases we make – and sometimes land ourselves in deeper trouble.

That trouble comes when we construct an image that's false or that we can't afford. We run into debt, living beyond our means, perhaps not even sharing the growing dilemma with our family. The results are well documented – loss of home, family break-up, depression, even suicide. How we are seen is so important that everything has been sacrificed on the altar of image. Indeed, religious imagery isn't inappropriate. A Christmas leaflet in Kent had the single word 'HEAVEN' emblazoned on the front. Inside was an advert for Ashford's out-of-town shopping centre. Consumer heaven is an all-embracing fantasy.

The situation isn't helped by an omnipresent advertising industry. Wherever we look we are being told what to buy. On TV, on the internet, in junk mail, on football pitches, on roadside hoardings, on the back of bus tickets – we're the subject of unrelenting pressure to buy goods we don't need for the sake of happiness that doesn't last. So far I've held out against electronic books for all kinds of practical as well as sentimental reasons, but I know my resistance is being undermined as the advertising process is wearing away at me, seducing me with advantages and offers. Ask me how I'm doing in a few months' time! Of course I value some advertising, particularly the adverts that make me laugh, and British adverts can be very funny indeed. But I know it's all part of the softening up. The bottom-line question still is: do I need this product?

Another major problem is the widespread exploitation of workers producing goods for Western markets in faraway countries. Even on the morning I'm writing this there was a news item on workers in India making clothes for some major high street stores in the UK. Here were female workers earning £36 for a month's work, six days a week, 12 hours a day. They were put up in hostels that felt like captivity and sometimes woken in the night to fulfil emergency orders. (Or so it was claimed.)[4] The Fairtrade movement and other programmes try with increasing success to address such issues, but the disease still breaks out elsewhere because it relates to one of the basic instincts of the human heart – greed.

How could we think about this?

We might begin by agreeing that image is indeed everything – but only if we're talking about the image of God. It's basic to a Christian understanding of what it is to be human that we are made in the image of God, and although that image may be marred and damaged, it's indelible (Genesis 1.27). What matters, therefore, isn't what we look like to our neighbours but what we look like to God, and God sees us with the satisfaction of the Creator who 'saw everything that he had made, and indeed, it was very good' (v. 31). Note the word 'very'. God is pleased as punch with each of us. We have intrinsic value, not a value created by our job, bank balance, looks or consumer choices. Yes, there is a subsequent story that we call the Fall, but the first word from God is one of pride and joy in us. I know just a fraction of that feeling when I think of my daughters and their children; however they might mess up (and they haven't), they are superb and I love them to bits. Our value lies in being made in the image of God, not in the image of a designer label.

'Why do you worry about clothing? Consider the lilies of the field, how they grow; they neither toil nor spin, yet I tell you, even Solomon in all his glory was not clothed like one of these' (Matthew 6.28, 29). Christians know these verses very well, but when we go into our favourite high street store do we have that thinking anywhere in mind? Fashion dictates many choices in the West. It's so easy to dispose of the old and tired; I look into my wardrobe and see masses of clothes I don't wear, mainly because I'm bored with them. But life isn't disposable and the world's resources aren't infinite. Christians above all ought to be aware that appearances aren't everything; what matters is character. On the other hand, God has given us the capacity for beauty, and even the poorest of people usually still want to make the most of their appearance. As ever, there is a balance to be found and, as ever, we in the West have often got it wrong.

It's important that Christians don't resist complexity in the business of shopping. Trying to shop ethically takes us into a labyrinth of decision-making. For example, we often say it's better to buy locally sourced food because that will be less profligate in carbon consumption. But it's actually up to four times more environmentally friendly in terms of carbon emissions to buy New Zealand-produced lamb than lamb from the UK because in New Zealand they use less intensive farming methods, have more natural feed (grass) and make much more use of renewable power.[5] Again, roses from Kenya, flown to the UK, typically have only a sixth of the total carbon footprint of Dutch imports.[6] Other issues give rise to similar complexity: the GM and organic issues, for example, are not easily sorted out by quick slogans. Shopping in a supermarket is an ethical nightmare when there are some 40,000 products on sale, with 600 kinds of coffee and 400 brands of shampoo (not all in the same store!). We mustn't be afraid of the complexity, but nor must we be innocent of it. Above all, Christians have a high principle to adhere to: 'Strive first for the kingdom of God and his righteousness' (Matthew 6.33). Put God and his desire for justice first, all the time. Everything else follows.

What could we do differently?

- One very practical thing we could do is look at our bank statement for the last month and evaluate the things we've bought. Was it what we needed or was it optional? Was it for ourselves or for others? Was it routine or exceptional? Was it in line with our beliefs and values? What would Jesus or a neighbour or someone from a developing country say about the purchases we've made? We don't need to be ashamed of spending the money we've earned; we just need to be thoughtful about how it takes leave of our bank balance.

- Another question to ask ourselves is whether we often buy on impulse. Impulse is sometimes a good guide because it corresponds to deeply held and trustworthy preferences. But on other occasions it's good to slow down the process of purchasing. I have a lovely cartoon of two penguins on a small ice floe, looking at a lawnmower. One penguin is saying to the other: 'OK, I admit it. It was an impulse buy.' My father-in-law, on the other hand, when buying anything of substance, will research it to death until he's absolutely sure he's got the best bargain for precisely what he wants. And I find that I often go into a favourite clothes or bookshop and very quickly see something that will make my life complete. On occasions I will then go away, visit other shops, and then return to the scene of the original sin and realize that the magic has gone and in fact I really don't need that object after all. Delay is a good strategy in responsible shopping.
- There are a number of policies we can adopt in order to shop more ethically. One is to have a preference for fair trade goods (see box). This doesn't solve all the problems but it ensures a degree of altruism and benefit to the producer. We can also resist buying goods we think are overpackaged, and we can make sure we take our own carrier bags. We can avoid designer labels and buy 'own brand' goods. We can be generous and buy goods for the local food bank, not forgetting the *Big Issue* seller at the door. Shopping faithfully can become quite an adventure.

Widely accepted criteria for fair trade[7]

A business that:

1   pays fair prices to producers;
2   supports producers in their social and environmental projects;
3   promotes gender equality in pay and working conditions;
4   advises on product development to increase markets;
5   commits to long-term relationships to provide stability;
6   campaigns to highlight inequalities in world trade that place profit above human rights and that threaten the environment.

- I've never actually tried this, but we could decide on a personal shopping fast one day a week or one weekend a month. Fasting tells us many things about ourselves . . .

They said this

I want it all, I want it now. (Rock group Queen)

In this new world everything is possible, and most of it is for sale.

(Alison Morgan)[8]

The world is one great object for our appetite, a big apple, a big bottle, a big breast; we are the sucklers, the eternally expectant ones, the hopeful ones, and the eternally disappointed ones.

(Erich Fromm)[9]

Taking it further

Anchor passage: Matthew 6.24–34
Read once, take a full two minutes to reflect, then read it again.

To think about

Opener: What are your weaknesses when it comes to shopping? Is that OK? (It might be – we mustn't be kill-joys.)

- Is v. 25 only appropriate for people in richer, developed societies? How would a herdsman in Ethiopia hear this?
- 'Do not worry, saying . . . "What will we wear?"' (v. 31). What is a reasonable Christian message to the fashion industry?
- What strategies of resistance do you have to cope with the assault of consumerism and blanket advertising?
- What does it really mean in day-to-day language to 'strive first for the kingdom of God' (v. 33)?

- 'My father's generation, they don't crave things like I do . . . People in my generation, we always want the next thing. It's how we express ourselves and live our dreams.' What would you say to that young Chinese man?

Prayer: Have the group get out some money so everyone is holding a note or coin. Using the imagination, discuss what those notes or coins might have done in their lifetime. Pray over the money, that it may be well used. Put the money into a bowl to give to a charity that you agree on over coffee.

9

Being political

The Prime Minister stood up in Christ Church Cathedral in Oxford and said plainly:

> I have never really understood the argument some people make about the Church not getting involved in politics. To me, Christianity, faith, religion, the Church and the Bible are all inherently involved in politics because so many political questions are moral questions. I certainly don't object to the Archbishop of Canterbury expressing his views on politics . . . but he shouldn't be surprised when I respond.[1]

What's the problem?

Unfortunately, not everyone sees it that way. Every time a bishop dares to say anything 'political' the cry goes up: 'Religious leaders should keep out of politics; it's nothing to do with them.' Meanwhile, those same religious leaders get increasingly exasperated because they can't see how it's possible *not* to see religion and politics as two lenses of the same pair of binoculars. As Archbishop Desmond Tutu memorably put it: 'I am puzzled about which Bible people are reading when they suggest religion and politics don't mix.' Mahatma Gandhi was just as forthright: 'I can say without the slightest hesitation, and yet in all humility, that those who say religion has nothing to do with politics do not know what religion means.'

A simplified analysis might go like this: on the political left, the voice of the Church is valued in relation to issues such as world poverty, race, immigration, the needs of children and so forth, while its voice on issues of individual morality is not so welcome. On the political right, in contrast, the Church's contribution to debates on individual morality is what counts, whereas what it says on poverty, race, asylum seekers and so on is less welcome. Hence the Church's suspicion that it might be getting it about right – we're offending just about everybody!

What makes the debate about faith and politics more complex is that there are clearly convinced Christian politicians of real integrity in every party. Moreover, there can be no simplistic 'reading-off' of political policies from the Bible. There are stories, principles, precepts, people struggling to make right decisions, but there is no simple 'this means that' in terms of specific policy-making. The water gets muddier still when strident religious campaigning groups start shouting crude slogans that catch the media's attention, while more nuanced theological discussion goes unnoticed because it's more complex and less obviously adversarial. The abortion debate has often gone this way, as have discussions on religious rights in relation to wearing a cross at work, or a doctor offering to pray with a patient.

How could we think about this?

In the first place it's important to remember that God creates and loves a material world, not a spiritual ghetto. Similarly, Jesus proclaimed a kingdom, not a religion. He never said he had come to found a new religion; rather, he came so that all people 'may have life, and have it abundantly' (John 10.10). This must mean the welfare and flourishing of all people in every dimension of their being, from the quality of their housing and opportunities for their employment, to the education of their children and provision for their leisure. As ever, the sacred–secular divide is an illusion.

It may also be necessary to remind ourselves that the Old Testament prophets were always in the thick of national politics. The relationships of Elijah with King Ahab, Nathan with King David and Amos with Jeroboam were, to say the least, robust. Their astringent commentary on the ethical and religious behaviour of kings and common people put them right at the heart of national life. And they were in no doubt that God's instructions were 'to do justice, to love kindness, and to walk humbly with [your] God' (Micah 6.8). True fasting was to 'loose the bonds of injustice, to undo the thongs of the yoke, to let the oppressed go free, and to break every yoke . . . to share your bread with the hungry, and bring the homeless poor into your house' (Isaiah 58.6, 7). There was no mincing of words; contemporary church reports would be unlikely to pass muster with Amos.

At the same time, Paul reminds his readers that our political leaders are God-given and deserving of respect, for 'there is no authority except from God, and those authorities that exist have been instituted by God . . . Rulers are not a terror to good conduct but to bad' (Romans 13.1, 3). Our responsibility, therefore, is to accept that 'supplications, prayers, intercession, and thanksgivings should be made for everyone, for kings and all who are in high positions, so that we may lead a quiet and peaceable life' (1 Timothy 2.1). This exhortation has proved challenging in many dark political periods, but Paul was quite experienced in political maltreatment and therefore was all the more conscious of the need for honest, just and wise rulers. He says, in effect: 'We need good order to live in God's way in God's world, so pray that our rulers may be the kind of rulers we need.' At the same time Christians remember Jesus' classic encounter with the Pharisees over whether they should pay taxes to Caesar. Jesus made it quite clear that although there is a proper authority carried by Caesar, ultimately God is our ruler and king: 'Give to God the things that are God's', that is, everything (Matthew 22.15–22). There are limits to human authority; there are no limits to God's. Where there is a clash, God wins.

We need also to recognize that Christians acting in the political sphere have often got it badly wrong as well as gloriously right. Examples of the former might be the dangerously theocratic government of Calvin's Geneva, or the theological backing the Dutch Reformed Church gave to apartheid in South Africa, or the more extreme rhetoric of the Christian right in the United States. Examples of the latter might be the faith-inspired social reformers in nineteenth-century Britain, the churches in South Africa and the USA that tackled racial injustice head on and the churches in Eastern Europe that were places of resistance and inspiration that led to the fall of communism. There is material in Christian history for both lamentation and gratitude, and we need to be honest about both.

What could we do differently?

- We could ask the question: 'Why do I vote as I do?' Most of us vote according to our instincts, shaped by our upbringing, class, education and so on. We could instead try to root our political decisions in our faith, to see how well they fit and if necessary to revise them. This is hard work because, as we have seen, our Christian sources remain ambiguous. However, the 'framing story' of the prophets, of Jesus' life, of the Beatitudes, of Paul's attempts to apply faith to daily life in the early church, is a vibrant story to inhabit, and from there to discern how adequately the various political manifestos overlap the defining story we have as Christians.

- We could ask another question: 'As an ordinary citizen, what could I do to improve some part of my community?' Implicitly, Christians are asking that question all the time because it's clear that, in very many communities, if all the Christians withdrew from local charities, welfare organizations and community groups, those organizations would collapse. However, church life is a greedy activity and the wider question of how we could change that bit of creation in which we are placed – our own locality – is an important one to ask ourselves if we are to fulfil Jesus' promise of a kingdom of love and justice, and not merely support a religious club for those who like that kind of thing. Could we contribute as a school governor, parish councillor, CAB volunteer, lunch-club cook, or in a computer drop-in centre, a playgroup, an ex-offender support programme? The list is endless.

- The same question should be asked of the church as a community, perhaps in the form: 'How can we be a blessing to the community around us?' (Or, more negatively, if this church weren't here, would the community notice?) When Barack Obama arrived in Chicago he joined a church because his boss told him that if he wanted to help the poor: 'The churches are the only game in town. That's where the people are, and that's where the values are, even if they've been buried under a lot of bullshit' (OK, point taken).[2] The church could do an audit of the local community and see where the gaps in provision are most obvious and attempt to meet them. One church in Abingdon supports a food bank, a financial advice centre, a drop-in for lonely people, an international café for overseas students and families, a prison ministry and street pastors. It's all an outworking of the belief that love has skin on it. It's real. It's practical.
- And some, I sincerely hope, may feel that their Christian commitment drives them to stand for council elections or even Parliamentary elections. This is where the hard work goes on, in committee and council, week in, week out, and where the plumb-line of a Christian world view is most valuable. If not you, who? Pray that God will call many to this discipleship, and pray for those who have accepted the challenge.

☆ *A new minister came to a church which he had been told was one of the most successful on the eastern seaboard of the United States. However, across the river was a shipyard where nuclear submarines were built and many of the congregation worked. The minister set up a study group to work at the connection between faith and the armaments industry. People were outraged at the group's report and the church divided; many left and church programmes declined. Some, however, caught a whiff of a new depth of discipleship and they began sharing more of their lives with each other, and then with the underprivileged in their own neighbourhood, and then with the poor in the developing world. The minister was asked to move and refused. Numbers fell to a quarter of what they had been. The death of the church seemed imminent. But then the new quality of life of the church began to attract others, even some of those who had previously left. It wasn't long before membership reached an all-time high with income three times what it had been. A church which had been a corporate chaplain to the arms industry had, by risking its own life, become a seed-bed for peace and justice.*[3]

- As a citizen of a world that's increasingly on our doorstep, what campaigning groups might we give time and effort to supporting? Of course many have Christian roots – Oxfam, Christian Aid, Tearfund, World Vision, Amnesty, A Rocha – but there are scores of others that clearly dovetail with the Christian agenda of a world enjoying the goodness of the Lord. How high are they as a priority in our pattern of discipleship? Do we give money? Can we give time?
- At the very least, will we watch and listen to the news with the eyes and ears of Christ? And will that lead us to pray? We are never helpless as Christians before the enormity of the world's needs; we have the mighty resource of prayer. Theologian Karl Barth said: 'To clasp the hands in prayer is the beginning of an uprising against the disorder of the world.'

They said this

When I give food to the poor, they call me a saint. When I ask why the poor have no food, they call me a communist.

(Dom Helder Camara, Archbishop of
Olinda and Recife)[4]

As the years of my premiership passed, one fact struck me with increasing force: that failure to understand the power of religion meant failure to understand the modern world. Religious faith and how it develops could be of the same significance to the 21st century as political ideology was to the 20th. Leaders, whether of religious faith themselves of not, have to 'do God'.

(Tony Blair, British Prime Minister 1997–2007)[5]

What if we replaced the dysfunctional categories of Left and Right, liberal and conservative, with two questions: what's right, and what works?

(Jim Wallis, leader of the Sojourners)[6]

Taking it further

Anchor passage: Matthew 22.15–22
Read once, take a full two minutes to reflect, then read it again.

To think about
Opener: Would you say that politics and your faith have come together at any particular time in your life?

- 'Give to the emperor the things that are the emperor's, and to God the things that are God's.' What does that really mean? What things are God's?
- In the parable of the Labourers in the Vineyard (Matthew 20.1–16), how do you evaluate the claims of justice and of grace? Can this parable and its message transfer into the political realm?
- Try to trace the root philosophy of each of the main political parties. Where do they overlap with Christian thinking? (Why do we find it hard to discuss politics in our churches?)
- What advice would you give the Archbishop of Canterbury in relating to government today?
- What could the churches do to encourage participation in politics, rather than just be polling stations in elections?

Prayer: Think of two or three of the key political dilemmas of the moment. Briefly discuss the different elements that make them difficult to resolve. Out of that discussion, pray for those situations and the people involved, perhaps allocating different aspects of them to different people.

10

Making peace

When we watch the average evening news broadcast we usually see a violent world reflected back at us. Sometimes we look on in amazement, wondering how human beings can do these things to each other. At other times we feel deeply sad that petty differences and jealousies can cause such violence when our fragile planet has so many more important issues to address. And on occasions we may even catch a glimpse of a darker truth – that the seat of this violence is in our own hearts, not just in the hearts of others.

There is violence in the home – a quarter of British women suffer domestic assault at some stage in their lives, and two women a week in the UK die of it.[1] There is violence on the streets – riots break out and all sorts of people are caught up in the frenzy. There is violence on our television screens and in our films. It's said that an American child will have seen 40,000 deaths on TV before he or she leaves primary school (mostly cartoon deaths, I imagine). There is violence notably in our video games, the scale of which is truly alarming. 'Welcome to 666 games,' says one internet advert. 'We serve you the most violent, brutal, sadistic and bloody flashgames on the internet.' It then adds, innocently: 'Always keep in mind it's just digital violence.'

Something very deep is going on here and Christians need to be aware of the complexity. 'The heart is devious above all else; it is perverse – who can understand it?' (Jeremiah 17.9).

What's the problem?

Humanity seems addicted to violence. Acts of aggression have always been the most frequent strategy for solving disputes. During the twentieth century, 43 million military personnel were killed in war, and 62 million civilians.[2] The United Nations estimates that every day over 1,000 innocent people are killed by conventional weapons, twice as many per year as were killed by the nuclear devices dropped on Hiroshima and Nagasaki.[3] And yet we talk endlessly of peace. Our hearts are divided.

Too often religion has played a part in the conflicts that have torn nations to pieces. The Church has justified killing and torture, encouraged violence and blessed wars. As Brian McLaren puts it: 'For every Martin Luther King and Desmond Tutu proclaiming the Jesus who rode on a donkey and spoke of peace, there have been plenty who proclaim a different Jesus, well armed and dangerous.'[4] Christians may try to wriggle round the charge but it's best to come clean and admit that there's a lot of unhealthy religion around, and always has been.

And yet evil has to be resisted. It's not acceptable to dress evil up in nice clothes and pretend it isn't what it is. The problem comes in knowing how far our own violence is justified in resisting the contorted face of evil. There is a noble history of non-violent resistance, demonstrated, for example, by Gandhi and Martin Luther King, but there is an equal theological tradition of the just war. How are Christians to make judgements in this complex ethical environment? Moreover, this is no armchair debate; innocent people are dying every day.

If violence has its roots deep in our hearts, then we're faced with the puzzle of how we change the human heart. Christians believe that it's possible in the transformation Christ offers, but the evidence is ambivalent. Jonathan Swift said: 'We have just enough religion to make us hate, but not enough to make us love one another.'[5] How can the soul be flooded with the peace of Christ so that the violence we carry evaporates?

How could we think about this?

We start with the *shalom* of God. This great Old Testament theme explores the wholeness and joy of a creation at peace with itself and with its Creator. It's not merely the absence of conflict but more positively the presence of an embracing peace and harmony. This *shalom* is given expression in the sabbath rest of God, in the ideal of Jubilee and in Isaiah's vision of the wolf living with the lamb and the leopard lying down with the kid (Isaiah 11.6). The new creation described poetically in Revelation is a world in which heaven and earth fully overlap each other and God's *shalom* is finally established. This is our destination and our desire, and what we desire we must work for.

The teaching of Jesus is full of challenge to a violent humanity. He calls peacemakers blessed, promising that they will be called children of God (Matthew 5.9). He states unequivocally that 'all who take the sword will perish by the sword' (Matthew 26.52). He sets before us the high challenge to love our enemies and to pray for those who persecute us (Matthew 5.44). What he doesn't recommend is superior fire-power. It's not surprising that there's an honourable tradition of pacifism in the Church, even though most Christians have still found ways of squaring their conscience with using force to resist the excesses of evil. Reflecting on Jesus' command to love our enemies, Archbishop Robert Runcie said: 'This saying is still offensive and obscure to many, but "love your enemies" is a credible peace strategy, and the only one the Church as such is authorised to pursue.'[6]

St Paul picked up the peacemaking theme with alacrity and declared peace with God and with each other to be a central part of the work of Christ. 'He came and proclaimed peace to you who were far off and peace to those who were near' (Ephesians 2.17). Paul's letters are full of his urging of believers to live at peace because he clearly saw that 'Christ is our peace ... he has made both groups into one, and has broken down the dividing wall' (Ephesians 2.14). This counter-cultural way of living at peace in a particularly violent age would have a dramatic effect on those who observed it. 'Look how they love one another and how they are ready to die for each other', was the astonished cry of outsiders.[7] If Christians can demonstrate the way of peace there's something immensely attractive to a world weary of conflict and violence. Other religious traditions have often been more successful at this. One cannot but feel awkward at the response of Gandhi to a journalist's question about what he thought of Western civilization. 'I think it would be a very good idea', he answered.

☆ *There was a terrifying warlord whose dreadful deeds went before him. The villages were evacuated as he stormed through the country-side. At the last village, however, he was told by his men that one old monk remained. He howled in rage and had the monk brought to him. 'Do you not know who I am?' he bellowed. 'I am he who can run you through with a sword and not even bat an eye.' The old monk looked up at him and said: 'And do you not know who I am? I am the one who can let you run me through with a sword – and never even bat an eye.'*[8]

What could we do differently?

- We could practise peace at home. If peace starts in the heart and the home then this is the place to rehearse the moves that make for peace further afield. Irritations can flare up into arguments and arguments into open warfare, be it of the trench warfare, sniping or hand-to-hand variety. Home is where peace strategies can be learnt – the value of deep listening, the importance of both contrition and forgiveness, the need for generous compromise, the necessity of not standing on dignity, and always to talk, talk, talk. Is there anyone at home with whom we are not at peace?
- We need to keep up a critique of violence in the regular diet of television programmes, films and video games that flood society.

The depiction of violence has escalated in recent years. Academics still debate the extent to which such stark representation damages the psychological well-being of young people, but common sense tells us there must be some effect. Or else why do companies pay such huge sums for advertising on TV? Nevertheless, Christians will want to be careful about those with whom they find themselves making common cause. Deeply conservative groups that advocate robust censorship may well be poor partners in the long run. Censorship is rarely a positive or long-lasting strategy, but educating our desires and advocating healthier models of entertainment is a worthwhile approach to take. This is where responsible support and encouragement of our MPs is crucial as they tackle the issues that shape society.

- We could also keep up a rigorous critique of violence as we encounter it on the news. Not to protest is to collude. Between 1950 and 1990 the United States and the Soviet Union between them amassed about 70,000 nuclear warheads whose combined power was one million times greater than the bomb that destroyed Hiroshima.[9] Not to protest at the madness of the MAD (mutually assured destruction) strategy would have been to accept the unacceptable. The invasion of Iraq, Israeli shelling of Gaza, Syrian treatment of its opposition, Iranian execution of its dissidents – all these have in recent years shocked the world and demanded its disapproval. Christians must always protest in the name of the Prince of Peace whose ways were so different. But how can we do that? In our conversations we can make sure we speak peace and don't submit to the rhetoric of violence. There are letters to write, groups to join, petitions to sign, votes to cast, perhaps marches to go on. History is full of the truth that small actions from many people make changes happen.
- Many organizations are committed to peacemaking and need intelligent support. The United Nations may often seem toothless in the face of determinedly oppressive regimes but it gathers and focuses international support for concerted pressure and we would be much the poorer without it. NGOs and charities such as Christian Aid, the Red Cross, Amnesty, Reprieve and very many others are all keeping

up the pressure for peace and need our support. And we should always be commending alternatives to the tired, familiar strategies of sabre-rattling and Russian roulette. As ever the key alternative is talking. As Moshe Dayan, the Israeli general and politician, once said: 'If you want to make peace you don't talk to your friends. You talk to your enemies.'

- Pray regularly for places of conflict and those who can bring peace there.

They said this

Peace is not merely the absence of tension, but the presence of justice.   (Martin Luther King)[10]

Achieve inner peace and thousands around you will be saved.
                                          (Seraphim of Sarov, 1759–1833)

A blackbird said to a dove: 'I sat on the branch of a fir, close to its trunk, when it began to snow. Since I didn't have anything better to do, I counted the snowflakes settling on the twigs and needles of my branch. There were exactly 3,741,952. When the next snowflake dropped on to the branch, the branch broke off.' The dove – since Noah's time an authority on the question of peace – thought about the story for a while and then said to the blackbird: 'Perhaps there is only one person's voice missing for peace to come about in the world.'
                                                                (Anon)

Taking it further

Anchor passage: Matthew 5.1–12
Read once, take a full two minutes to reflect, then read it again.

To think about
Opener: What did you do when you were last seriously angry with someone? What did you learn from that?

- Should we see the Beatitudes as an aspiration, straightforward policy, exaggeration for the sake of emphasis, a picture of the kingdom, or what?
- When have the meek inherited the earth?
- Who are the peacemakers you most admire, or have done in the past?
- How strong is the case for pacifism?
- What does loving your enemy mean in world politics? Be specific in terms of contemporary conflicts.
- Take a world trouble-spot and analyse the issues involved in making peace. Do the same with any conflict you may have experienced in church life.

Prayer: Take a map of the world and place night lights on trouble-spots, lighting the candle and praying for the country and its people as each candle is placed on the map.

11

Doing justice

History says that I failed my GCE history exam. I know I didn't. I always came top in history; I loved it. In the mock exams I got 92 per cent and I did an even better paper in the real exam. But I was given a fail, together with the entire class (which was absurd), and no amount of appealing to the examination board could get them to admit that their first year of using a computer had led to a major mistake. You can tell I'm still cross.

There's a deep instinct in the human heart about fairness. Listen to the children of any family discussing anything from the distribution of sweets to the amount of their pocket money and you'll hear the cry go up: 'It's not fair.' There seems to be a balancing mechanism inside us that insists on fairness. And what starts in our personal make-up stretches out to embrace a world of inequalities. We bridle at minor injustice and are outraged at major failures of the system. It's all of a piece. As Martin Luther King said: 'Injustice anywhere is a threat to justice everywhere.' No one should be more concerned with justice than one who believes in God.

What's the problem?

The inequalities we tolerate across the whole planet are extraordinary. The richest 1 per cent of the world's population owns 40 per cent of its wealth, and 10 per cent own 85 per cent. At the other extreme, 50 per cent of the world's adults own just 1 per cent of its wealth[1] and 2.5 billion people live on less than $2 per day. The wealth of the world's three richest *individuals* is greater than the combined GDP of the world's 48 poorest *countries*. Half a per cent of the money the USA spends on its military budget would cut hunger in Africa in half.[2] These jaw-dropping statistics go on and on. Moreover, in their influential book, *The Spirit Level*, Richard Wilkinson and Kate Pickett demonstrate that almost every modern social problem, from ill-health, violence and obesity to mental illness, drugs and crime, is more likely to occur in a less equal society. Inequality is bad for the world's health.[3]

The international community plans – and practically always fails – to address these deep inequalities. The Millennium Development Goals were set by world leaders in 2000 in order to eradicate extreme poverty by 2015. There has been progress, but overall the high hopes of the millennium have been dashed. It has been the same in a series of global conferences on climate change. Kyoto led to Bali, which led to Copenhagen and then to Rio. We look for a global will to take seriously enough the question of the survival of the planet, but we look in vain. Self-interest is always the stumbling block.

It's hard to get round the road block of self-interest. When our own interests are securely set on the throne of our lives, it takes something enormous to make them move out. Self-interest has a number of cognates – self-centredness, self-regard, self-absorption, self-aggrandizement, self-indulgence, self-righteousness, self-seeking and so on. None of them is very attractive; all of them are common to humankind. And if justice is to prevail, the dominance of self-interest has to be overthrown.

How could we think about this?

God is passionate about justice. His prophets, biblical and post-biblical, have always made justice their prime concern. 'Let justice roll down like waters, and righteousness like an ever-flowing stream,' thundered

Amos (5.24). 'What does the LORD require of you but to do justice, and to love kindness, and to walk humbly with your God,' wrote Micah (6.8). 'Is not this the fast that I choose: to loose the bonds of injustice, to undo the thongs of the yoke, to let the oppressed go free . . . ?' demanded Isaiah (58.6). I have a version of the Bible that highlights in blue every verse that relates to God's desire to give his people freedom from oppression and injustice. Practically every one of its 1,200 pages has blue highlights.[4] On a bad day I despair of the way we Christians have obsessed about relatively minor causes based on sparse biblical evidence when the great bell of the Bible is ringing in our ears with God's passion for justice.

Jesus of course shared this concern and reserved his sharpest tongue for the religious and civil authorities who oppressed the poor. His most violent act was to create mayhem with the stalls of those who were raking off a juicy profit from poor worshippers. But Jesus went even further. He took justice and equity as a baseline and then broke through it into a new economy of grace. The labourers who were paid the same for their one hour's work as those who'd worked all day were the recipients not of a wooden form of 'just reward' but of a new order of generosity. In God's kingdom we aren't all levelled down to a system of tariffs but levelled up to a world of unimaginable gift and grace. Which world would you rather belong to, asks Jesus (Matthew 20.1–16). And how far are we prepared to inhabit this uncharted territory?

Jesus spoke a lot about what he called the kingdom of God. It wasn't a phrase used by many biblical figures either before or after him; it was very much his own category and therefore highly significant. Jesus was deliberately opaque about its meaning, and used the phrase in different ways, offering his hearers pictures to illustrate what the kingdom might be, rather than conceptual definitions that might have restricted it. Matthew 13, for example, is full of such pictures. But if we are to be boring twenty-first-century pedants, what might the phrase mean? Perhaps we could think of the kingdom of God as the arena where God's will is sought, enjoyed and obeyed. It's wherever God's values are operating. The Franciscan writer Richard Rohr speaks of the kingdom as being the Big Picture of how things really are, objectively, truly and finally. The inside of things is always bigger than the merely outside, he says, and Jesus is always inviting us into this Big Picture.[5] However we describe the kingdom of God, it certainly exhibits the nature and qualities of God and is therefore characterized by justice, grace and love. Justice is non-negotiable for a Christian.

The kingdom

It's a long way off but inside it
There are quite different things going on:
Festivals at which the poor man
Is king and the consumptive is
Healed; mirrors in which the blind look
At themselves and love looks at them
Back; and industry is for mending
The bent bones and the minds fractured
By life. It's a long way off, but to get
There takes no time and admission
Is free, if you will purge yourself
Of desire, and present yourself with
Your need only, and the simple offering
Of your faith, green as a leaf.

(R. S. Thomas)[6]

What could we do differently?

- We could always be on the lookout for signs of the kingdom with which we can identify and that we can support. It's important to emphasize that they don't need to have a Christian label. God doesn't go in for labels but for realities. Where there are signs of grace that liberate, reconcile, create, serve, build community, nurture compassion, relish the natural world and so on, we may be sure that God is at work and the kingdom is present. On the other hand, when we encounter things that oppress, isolate, bind, sow enmity, create loneliness, produce egotism, demand idolatry and so forth, you may be sure that the kingdom is absent and God needs allies to work with him to turn the situation around. We need to be sensitive to the deeper architecture of the situations we occupy and encounter, in order to serve the kingdom well.

- This awareness may well lead us into social and political involvement. John Ruskin wrote: 'If you do not wish for [God's] Kingdom, don't pray for it. But if you do, you must do more than pray for it; you must work for it.'[7] I'm always delighted when I discover Christians who are involved as local councillors, who have let their faith drive them into standing for a council seat in order to make a difference. It may mean less churchgoing but more gospel-living, and that's entirely to be welcomed. Christians are always deeply involved in the work of local and national charities, but I find it's too easy to buy off my conscience with a direct debit. What matters just as much as giving money is taking an informed interest, praying and getting involved – getting on the streets in Christian Aid Week, writing letters for Amnesty, helping a recently discharged prisoner, visiting a lonely neighbour. Our task is to help to repair the world, and like any community project (though this one is rather large!) it has its own rewards. As Lionel Blue delightfully puts it: 'Do something for the sake of heaven, and heaven happens.'[8]

- There are many grey issues of justice about which we need to be honest with ourselves and honest to God. What about the black economy in which the purchaser pays less and the low-paid avoid tax? What about illegal music downloads, now so rampant in society that the law seems to have been left behind? What about the unrestrained leaking of confidential papers, a commonplace activity that breaks trust and yet makes organizations more accountable? These are issues that leave space for debate even if the pure moral principle is clear. Justice is sometimes a more nuanced concept than a black-and-white moral judgement.

- Could we get our church to take seriously the task of making a difference in our community? Look at the agenda of the church council and see how much of it is concerned with life outside the sacred walls. Some churches manage a rich social programme. Others may need to be encouraged to see that justice starts at home, both in the church (Who makes the decisions? Who never gets heard?) and in the immediate community. It's not just an issue for politicians and international conferences. Some implications are suggested in this book in Chapter 9, 'Being political' (p. 80). The starting point is believing, with Abraham Kuyper, that: 'There is not a square inch in the whole domain of our human existence over which Christ, who is sovereign over all, does not say: "This is mine".'[9]

- Many of the issues discussed in other chapters of this book raise questions of justice. Shopping raises questions about fair trade and the role of multinationals. Handling our sexuality raises questions about the exploitation of women. Handling money raises questions about corruption, tax avoidance, income inequality and corporate excess. Environmental concerns raise questions about the poorest paying the price of international self-interest. And so on. No wonder the Bible rings with a concern for justice.

They said this

Those who live in the light of the coming kingdom live in practical opposition to things as they are . . . Their challenge to the world, like that of Jesus himself, must always be an agonised cry: 'How can you do things this way, if God is who he is?'   (John V. Taylor)[10]

He who seeks first the Kingdom of God will have some problems, but he who seeks the Kingdom of God second, will have nothing but problems.   (Henry Drummond)

Taking it further

Anchor passage: Micah 6.6–end
Read once, take a full two minutes to reflect, then read it again.

To think about
Opener: Where and when has the injustice of the world come home to you most vividly?

- 'With what shall I come before the LORD . . . ? Shall I come before him with burnt-offerings, with calves a year old?' (v. 6). What are our modern equivalents?
- How could we put bones on God's requirements of justice, kindness and humility (v. 8), both individually and as a church?
- 'Can I tolerate wicked scales . . . ? Therefore I have begun to strike you down' (vv. 11–13). Is there a relationship between this kind of warning and the contemporary crises in the environment, the financial system, and food production?
- What chance is there of a world that goes beyond justice and into grace and generosity? Is that utopian? Can the Church live that way?

Prayer: Produce (or draw) a pair of old-fashioned scales. Name and place on one side the problems you have been identifying. Then name and place on the other side the character and gifts of God, placing each with prayer. Then each person covenant to undertake one action for justice before reporting back on it next week. Pray for courage!

PART 4

Facing others

———•◆•———

When we're trying to live faithfully we can get away with many deficiencies in the public sphere that are bound to show up in the personal sphere. How we relate to others in lifelong partnerships and friendships, and in living in close community, is a revealing test of our discipleship. Living faithfully requires us to handle personal relationships with real sensitivity, and perhaps, in that context, to share the most important dimensions of our lives, such as our faith.

12

Being attentive

———◆◆◆———

I wonder if you have been at a social gathering or a reception and found yourself with someone who clearly wasn't interested in talking to you. You try to find a way into a conversation but he's looking into his wine glass or over your shoulder, obviously hoping someone more significant will appear so he can excuse himself and depart. You want to say: 'Excuse me, I'm over here,' but you're not sure he'll hear even that pointed reminder. It's a demoralizing experience that can only be broken by robust means, such as mentioning in passing that you're thinking of becoming a sword-swallower, or some other extravagant disclosure.

What's the problem?

As a society we seem to find it extremely difficult simply to be present. We find it hard to focus on the present moment and the person or situation there before us. We want to be off to the next event, searching restlessly for experiences that will slake our thirst for fresh diversions. For us, this means skimming over the opportunities of the moment, and for the other person it means being left hurt by the roadside, dismissed as extraneous, surplus to requirements. It comes from living in a society that has become increasingly instrumentalist, where people are valued in work for their productivity, and in private life for their value to me and my interests. The end result is the apocryphal tale of the letter that started: 'Dear 3428634/A, We have a personal interest in you . . .'

Among clergy, this is pastorally disastrous. If ministers become known as clergy who don't bring their complete attention to the person before them, they'll soon find themselves having functional relationships rather than deep encounters. They may be admired and respected but they won't be loved, or even consulted. If I could give every newly ordained person one gift for ministry it would be the gift of attentiveness, for that attitude of heart and mind lies at the core of every human encounter of value. It's a gift but it's also a discipline, and one of the most urgent, if we are all, lay and ordained, to be true followers of Jesus in daily life.

How could we think about this?

It all starts with self-awareness. How aware am I of how I come across in human relationships? Do people find me interested, genuine, focused, caring, or detached, self-absorbed, careless with their feelings? Do I tend to give answers before I've heard the problem? Am I too dominant in conversation, not leaving space for others, or too reticent, failing to encourage others to open up? Some quiet reflection before God or some careful feedback from a caring partner or friend can help here, as can some honest journaling. Our capacity for self-deception is huge, so we need help in seeing ourselves with a clear eye. A man with marriage difficulties went to see a wise counsellor who said he must listen to his wife. He returned a month later to say he had listened to everything she had to say. The counsellor said with a smile: 'Now go and listen to every word she isn't saying.'

If we reflect on the way Jesus encountered people in need, it's clear he attended acutely to what people were both saying and not saying. When he met a woman who had come to a village well at midday (to avoid having to meet the other women of the community) he entered a deep conversation with her and soon realized that she was coming from a distressing series of relationships that had left her confused and demeaned. He helped her through to healing and hope for her future (John 4.1–42). He was so aware of what was going on around him that when a woman with gynaecological problems just touched his coat in a desperate attempt to find healing, he stopped and asked who it was, even though he was in the middle of a great crowd of people who were pressing in on him (Mark 5.21–34). In the garden after his resurrection he met Mary Magdalene and simply called her by name, knowing that her name, spoken by him, represented all that she needed to remind her of the confident identity and sense of self-worth that he had restored to her (John 20.11–18). Always, it seems, Jesus managed to so attune himself to the other person that he got under the surface of the presenting situation to the real issue beyond. Could we seek to emulate that?

It can be salutary to remember times when we've been put down or not listened to and how we felt about that experience. Many people live with self-doubt, and some with cripplingly low self-esteem. It doesn't take much to wipe the floor with their confidence, and the destroyer may never know it. If that has ever happened to us it can be wise to reflect on that incident and the impact it made on us, both at the time and subsequently. We don't want to pass that experience on to others.

☆ *I once used a machine that was supposed to test my personality. I put in my money, clung on to a handle and after a while a card emerged with the following text: 'Admirers have a high regard for your warm and loving personality. Your character is one that inspires trust. Great strength of purpose is apparent to all. Your artistic appreciation shows clarity of vision. [I was becoming very impressed with the perspicacity of this machine.] With such confidence you cannot help but succeed. Remember, becoming bald doesn't really matter.' [The machine was no longer in favour.]*

What could we do differently?

What follows applies, I believe, to a wide range of conversations in work settings, church meetings, pastoral conversations, coffee with friends and so on. It's about self-awareness leading to other-awareness, and therefore to the crucial gift of attentiveness.

- It may sound terribly pious, and I certainly don't always do it, but it helps before meeting someone to pray for a moment that you'll be able to see Christ in them and to see *what's really going on* in the conversation you're about to have. This doesn't mean that every functional encounter we have needs special prayer, but such prayer before conversations that have some substance puts the exchanges into a bigger context and opens them up to a three-way engagement (me–you–God) and a richer outcome.
- A really useful approach to take to any encounter like this is to ask the question beforehand: 'What's likely to be uppermost in this person's mind, or life, at the moment?' This flips the meeting over so that we enter it wanting to make contact with the other person's concern rather than simply our own agenda. We all carry so much emotional freight, and so many pressures and concerns, that the likelihood is we'll see our encounters through the lens of our own needs, with the result that we know at the end of the conversation that something was missing and we didn't quite meet each other. We find ourselves uneasy – but quickly move on to the next 'not quite right' encounter. Setting out to see the meeting through the eyes of the other person is a very useful corrective to this self-absorption.
- When talking to others, eye contact often means heart contact. Nothing is more reassuring to someone we're talking to than that we look at them. This doesn't mean staring at them unblinkingly, which may make them afraid of undisclosed homicidal tendencies, but it does mean we're staying with them and following their mind and their mood. And it's not just a technique; it also means we'll pick up clues that help us to understand what's going on and to be more receptive and responsive. For some of us this has to be a learnt skill because it doesn't come naturally, but it's distinctly worthwhile.

- We give off messages very early in a conversation. Our smile, hand-shake, warmth, interest, use of the person's name and so on give off important messages that put people at their ease and open up possibilities. It's all part of being attentive to the other and seeking their good. We then continue to try and 'read' the conversation, to be aware of both their responses and ours, so that there's reality and depth, openness and integrity in the exchange. Small things matter.
- The careful and gracious use of questions is a very significant way of valuing people and making a meeting with them both enjoyable and constructive. Jesus asked questions constantly. To the troubled demoniac: 'What's your name?' To blind Bartimaeus: 'What do you want me to do for you?' To the religious elite: 'Is it lawful to do good or to do harm on the sabbath?' To the disciples: 'Who do you say that I am?' To a lawyer: 'Which of these three do you think was a neighbour to the man who fell into the hands of the robbers?' To the couple trudging to Emmaus: 'What are you discussing with each other as you walk along?' Questions show interest, open up engagement and put the other person in the driving seat. They give value to the other person and enable us to get in touch with that person's reality rather than our fantasy about him or her. Of course it can be overdone and can pin the other person to the chair. It was once observed to me by a colleague that my questions over lunch had left him feeling like an onion being progressively peeled away, while giving nothing of myself. It was a salutary lesson, but born of genuine interest. I try to be more balanced now, but questions remain a generous way of giving attention to the other person and learning how to care.

They said this

We find it so difficult to become inwardly gathered, intent and still. Because we are for ever whisking through the present moment we almost never live in it. We are like champion sprinters in the hundred metres race, leaning forward, pushing our centre of gravity several

yards ahead, so that if we suddenly became still we should fall flat
on our faces. So the world around us, the reality of this present
moment, is blurred, unclear, empty in fact, because we have already
left it behind.   (John V. Taylor)

I confess to inwardly groaning sometimes as a new client comes to
see me. The thought of the many hours which we will spend in each
other's company over the coming months can initially fill me with
despair. However, without fail, as they share with me the reality of
their lives, I come to love them, not because I'm a spectacularly
loving person (far from it!) but because the process of giving
attention to people, people whom you believe to be made in the
image of God, and therefore to be loveable, enables you to come to
love them . . . As I have offered the gift of my attention to them I have
come to respect and admire them and to understand that they, in
their particular circumstances, have made a far better job of their
life than I in the same circumstances could have made.
                                      (Judy Hirst, ordained counsellor)[1]

Every person is Christ for me, and since there is only one Jesus,
that person is the one person in the world at that moment.
                                                        (Mother Teresa)

Taking it further

Anchor passage: Mark 5.1–20
Read once, take a full two minutes to reflect, then read it again.

To think about
Opener: Who of your friends and family gives you the best attention?
How does that show itself? And what's the consequence for you?

- What's the significance of Jesus asking the demoniac: 'What's your
  name?'

- 'He lived among the tombs; and no one could restrain him.' Who do we dismiss in our society or church as not really worth listening to?
- Jesus may have attended well to the mentally ill man but he didn't give much attention to the owners of the pigs, or the man himself when he wanted to go with Jesus. Did he attend selectively?
- What could you do to improve your listening and attentiveness skills? (Perhaps practise now by being in threes, one listening to another on a current issue he or she faces for five minutes and the third observing the process and feeding back afterwards. Then move round and repeat.)
- Is there a way your church could offer good listening to those in need of it, such as Listening Post coffee mornings, pastoral visiting team, bereavement team, lunch club, groups on oral history?

Prayer: Give thanks and pray for the situations and people who have been mentioned in the session so far. (This will show how well we have been listening and attending to what others have said!) Celebrate all that has been good. Pray for all the issues that need attention.

13

Being married

I once saw a Valentine's card that said on the front: 'I'd slay dragons for you.' Inside it said: 'Well, perhaps not slay them, but I'd certainly verbally abuse them on your behalf.'

There's a perennial crisis in relationships because we're not very well prepared for the range of emotional and practical responses we need to make in order to live closely with another person. We learn it on the hoof; we learn it by making mistakes; and most riskily of all, we learn it from a script given to us by our parents. The way our parents related to each other is a fundamental influence on how we handle our most intimate and intense relationships. The evidence is growing that as a society we're becoming increasingly confused about how to live well together. And yet the drive to find a life partner in whom to invest all our hopes is still immensely strong and the rewards are huge.

I once visited a man whose wife had just died. In the last ten years of their long married life he had never been away from her for longer than six hours – when he went to play bowls and stayed for a drink. He told me that when they were in their 80s they had been in a local park on a Sunday afternoon when a band struck up a familiar tune from the bandstand, so they got up and did a foxtrot on the grass. He said: 'I loved every breath she took.'

What's the problem?

Around 230,000 couples get married in the UK each year (400,000 in 1971), but 120,000 get divorced. The average length of a marriage now is 11.4 years and one in three marriages will be over by the fifteenth anniversary.[1] The NSPCC estimate that one in four children will experience the separation of their parents during childhood (one in 14 in 1972). The alternative to marriage has been a vast increase in cohabitation, which rose by 65 per cent between 1996 and 2006; 16 per cent of all couples were cohabiting by 2006.[2] Cohabitation doesn't seem to be a long-term answer, however, because the average length of such a relationship is only about seven years. In the meantime those who cohabit are less healthy and less wealthy, and their relationships are less stable and less faithful than couples who marry. And their children are only half as likely as the children of married couples to live their whole childhood with their natural parents.[3] We're still looking for the most effective ways to relate well to each other in deep relationships.

Statistics are deceptive: it's real people who get hurt when relationships don't work out. Perhaps we invest more in the nuclear family than it can bear. The extended family and the community support of older cultures spread the weight more widely so that couples didn't need to look for all their needs to be met in a single intense relationship. Of course, 'till death us do part' was also a much shorter time in previous centuries than it is now, when people may be married for over seventy years.

Moreover, in a society obsessed with feelings, we may have a higher threshold of what we expect from our key relationships than previous generations, and if we fail to receive the satisfaction we expect we may be tempted to start again with a new relationship. Our understanding of the different dimensions of love may be undeveloped and so we may only look at our relationships through the lens of immediate emotional satisfaction. That pressure is increased massively if we have an undiluted diet of celebrity magazines and television shows with their heavy investment in the regularly changing romantic partnerships of the wealthy and glamorous.

☆ *A husband and wife drove for miles in silence after a terrible argument in which neither would budge. The husband pointed to a mule in a field. 'Relative of yours?' he asked. 'Yes,' she replied. 'By marriage.'*

How could we think about this?

Perhaps we could start with a reconsideration of the nature of love. In English we only have one word for love; the Greeks wisely had four. *Storge* is affection-love, especially between family members, and is the natural fondness that comes from familiarity. *Philia* is friendship-love and a particularly profound expression of love because it's freely chosen. *Eros* is romantic love that longs for emotional connection. *Agape* is unconditional love that cares for others regardless of circumstance and is the most distinctively Christian form of love.

It's easy to see that our culture has invested heavily in *eros* but even *eros* has been stripped of its mystery. I cherish a definition of love that came from a psychiatrist at a conference. He declared: 'Love is the cognitive-affective state, characterized by intrusive and obsessive fantasizing, concerning reciprocity of amorant feeling by the object of the amorance.' I'm sure that's true, but I can vouch for it not being well received by one's wife. In any case, *eros*-love needs to be filled out with *agape*, *storge* and *philia* if it's to fulfil its potential and withstand the pressures of a trivializing culture.

It should be clear that the idea of love is a moving target, but a Christian approach will be rooted in the fundamental conviction that it's God himself who is the source of love, and it's from that grounding that the various dimensions, tones and textures of love emerge. 'God is love, and those who abide in love abide in God, and God abides in them' (1 John 4.16). That verse is regularly used to open a marriage service in church. Another passage often follows and that's the familiar hymn to love in 1 Corinthians 13, the middle section of which has much common sense for marriage, which needs ample generosity in *eros*, *philia*, *storge* and *agape*.

Love is patient; love is kind; love is not envious or boastful or arrogant or rude. It does not insist on its own way; it is not irritable or resentful; it does not rejoice in wrongdoing, but rejoices in the truth. It bears all things, believes all things, hopes all things, endures all things.   (vv. 4–7)

It would be good to print that passage out and stick it on the fridge.

What we learn especially from this is that love is intensely practical and has to be deeply resilient. Love is like a glass: it shatters if you hold it too tightly and it shatters if you hold it too loosely and drop it. But it's rooted in God, who never fails in love. Indeed, we could say that we can be absolutely certain that God's love is absolutely certain, and that allows our own love for our special partner to breathe and change and develop. Love should be second nature to us because it's the first nature of God. Love is the projection into the world of what God is, and because we are made in the image of God, love should define us too.

What could we do differently?

- It helps if we always try and keep our key relationship on a 'we' basis. By that I mean we should always start out with the conviction that we stand together, not as well-meaning, caring, but differentiated individuals. In that sense, 'we' take on the world. It's quite a good test of our core relationship to ask, figuratively speaking, are we shoulder to shoulder and in this together, or are we at an angle, looking askance at our partner and ready to distance ourselves a little when we're with others?
- We could make sure we give each other room to grow. Too many relationships fail because one partner can't conceive of the other becoming different, gaining new interests, new qualifications and new friends. Perhaps the fact that in 68 per cent of divorces it's the woman who initiates the process suggests that men often find the personal development of their partner difficult to accept. But 'love is kind; love is not envious . . . It does not insist on its own way'.
- There are certain key gifts that are more than words and need to be realities in a growing, breathing, healthy relationship. Gifts like honesty, thoughtfulness and generosity of spirit. But discipline comes

into it too. The discipline of laughter. The discipline of conflict resolu-
tion. (One couple said they heeded the biblical injunction never to
go to bed angry – but once they had to stay up for three weeks.) The
discipline of time given just to the other. My wife and I always try
to have a monthly treat booked in a long time ahead and therefore
a clear diary commitment. It could be a concert, a theatre outing, a
visit to friends, a holiday – but something that insists we take time
to be a couple and not just people who share a home.

- If 'education, education, education' is the mantra of successive governments, 'communication, communication, communication' ought
to be the mantra of every marriage or partnership. The language
of violence is all too common as couples lack the skills to relate in
constructive ways. Instead we need the gentler language of attention,
and the special language of touch. God made us to be physical beings
and honoured that in the Incarnation. Babies need to be held, lovers
need to kiss, partners need to be stroked, the dying need a holding
hand. Touch is important if we are to stay 'in touch' with each other.

- If possible, pray together. This can range from reading a Bible passage
in bed in the morning to saying Compline together at night. Our patterns of prayer are uniquely our own and may not combine easily
with our partner's, but even occasional praying together strengthens
the ties that bind.

They said this

I, N, take you, N, to be my [spouse], to have and to hold from this
day forward; for better, for worse, for richer, for poorer, in sickness
and in health, to love and to cherish, till death us do part; according
to God's holy law. In the presence of God I make this vow.

(*Common Worship* Marriage Service)

To know oneself half of a true pair, certain of its purity and integrity,
and the whole encompassed by warmth and tenderness, compassion,
pity and gratitude; this is the only way of overcoming our loneliness.

(Petru Dumitriu)[4]

Love is not love
which alters when it alteration finds,
or bends with the remover to remove.
O no, it is an ever-fixed mark
that looks on tempests and is never shaken.
(Shakespeare)[5]

Taking it further

Anchor passage: 1 Corinthians 13
Read once, take a full two minutes to reflect, then read it again.

To think about
Opener: Think of a successful marriage you know reasonably well (not your own if you're married). What do you think are the factors that have made it succeed?

- 'Love is not irritable or resentful' (v. 5). The people we know best often irritate us most. How can we counteract this human frailty? (Give examples if you dare!)
- 'Love bears all things, believes all things, hopes all things, endures all things' (v. 7). How can we bring that wonderful language down to earth? What would it mean in a key, intimate relationship?
- What would be the group's ten top guidelines for a successful lifelong partnership? Write them up.
- What do you think will happen to the patterns of marriage, partnership and intimate relationships in the next 20 years? What trends and swings would you expect? What can the Church do most effectively in that context?

Prayer: Each person is given a night light and asked to list out loud the marriages, civil partnerships and special relationships with which he or she is most involved. Light the candle, pray silently over the list. The leader reads some of the prayers from the marriage service.

14

Nurturing friendships

———·•◆•·———

Conventional wisdom says there's nothing better than a friend, unless it's a friend with chocolate. Good friends give life ballast and security when the rest of life is slipping off course. We may be right when we sing 'What a friend we have in Jesus' but we need that friendship to be made flesh as well. A friend is someone who knows nearly everything about you and still stands by you.

Friends emerge unexpectedly from many corners of life. C. S. Lewis said: 'Friendship is born at that moment when one person says to another: "What! You too? I thought I was the only one."[1] Suddenly you realize someone else occupies the same thought-space. You understand each other without having to argue a case. And sometimes it's sufficient just to be together.

> Piglet sidled up to Pooh from behind.
> 'Pooh?' he whispered.
> 'Yes, Piglet?'
> 'Nothing,' said Piglet, taking Pooh's hand. 'I just wanted to be sure of you.'[2]

What's the problem?

The Mental Health Foundation report for 2010 said that loneliness in the UK has reached epidemic proportions. A third of us don't know who our neighbours are. Thirty per cent of people live alone, and although that doesn't equate with loneliness, it could be the start. Indeed, at least 10 per cent of the population self-identify as lonely. There are many reasons – increased social mobility, moving for education or employment, the increased number of divorces, the restlessness of the culture. There are stereotypes of course – the loner male who has an obsession with video games, the Bridget Jones female looking desperately for a man – but loneliness is no respecter of stereotypes. It's much more diverse and complex. Some singles are very fulfilled with a chosen or accepted lifestyle; others would love to have a partner but won't accept second best. Some have come out of a relationship that has spoiled them for another, while others have come out too damaged to risk another. As the film title said: *It's Complicated*. Whether for good or ill it remains true that on average we live two-thirds of our lives as single people.

Male–female friendship has become both much easier and much more complex. Gender barriers in education have largely disappeared and social interaction is more relaxed. Such friendships can be enormously enjoyable as different perceptions weave a rich fabric of relationship that feels different from same-sex friendships. Nevertheless, because of the sexualization of all adult relationships in our culture, there's often considerable confusion about how male and female are to relate if not as a couple. Can they go out for a drink as they would with someone of the same sex? What are the limits of physical contact? Do they relate according to their own integrity or according to the suspicions of others? Are they deceiving themselves that it's just friendship? There can be considerable awkwardness and self-consciousness in male–female friendship.

When two lives come together with a degree of permanence, it's bound to have some effect on friendships. A man used to going out with his friends at the weekends has to reassess his priorities; a woman who made her own social calendar now has to consult her partner. If a balance isn't found, this can lead to social isolation, both for the couple and eventually for the solitary friend left metaphorically in the pub when all the others have paired off and gone. Friendship has a wider value than as a vehicle to get us to coupledom.

Best friend test: put your dog and your friend in the boot of the car for an hour. When you open the boot again, note who's really happy to see you.

How could we think about this?

In the second creation story in Genesis 2 we have God uttering the haunting phrase: 'It is not good that the man should be alone' (v. 18). It's not. We need friends, family, community. And God blesses Adam with a partner. It's just a start, but it leads on to the network of relationships that sustains us all. It's not good that we should be alone. We become morose or depressed or de-socialized. Solitary confinement is one of the most damaging experiences we can inflict on one another.

It's important, however, to distinguish loneliness from solitude. The latter is chosen, embraced and may offer a deep cleansing of the soul. Issues are clarified, priorities identified, society's rubbish is cleared away. I once went to the Shetlands to write a book. In those windswept islands, far from the plastic distractions of the mainland, I established a simple rhythm of writing, walking, eating, sleeping and praying. It was as if my life had been scoured of the glitzy accretions of a Western lifestyle and I had been put back in touch with the elements, with earth, wind and fire. But eventually I needed my family. We probably all need more solitude in our noisy, overfilled lives, but loneliness is different. God doesn't intend us to be alone.

Friendship is a key that fits the lock of Christian faith almost perfectly. Indeed, a friend of mine uses the theme of friendship as a way of explaining God's Big Story to children. It goes like this (with some of my own variations):

- making friends – the creation
- friends fall out – the Fall

- friends keep trying – the story of Israel
- the best, best friend – Jesus
- friends together – the Church
- friends forever – the new creation.

The whole biblical narrative can be seen as God searching out his people in order to bring them back into friendship, the friendship that from his side never wavered.

The culmination of the story is in the life of Jesus, who gathered a small group of friends, both male and female, and took them with him for the time of their lives. I like to think of the many hours they spent walking the hills and paths of Galilee, chatting, joking, playing touch rugby, barbecuing on the beach. A young man with his friends, purposeful and focused, but also enjoying the riches and rewards of friendship. And he was specific about his relationship with them: 'I have called you friends, because I have made known to you everything that I have heard from my Father' (John 15.15). He had shared everything with his friends, as friends do. And now he laid down his life for his friends.

It follows that the Church, which inevitably came into being after his departure, should be a network of the friends of Jesus – whether those friends had known Jesus in the flesh or in his risen life. The Church is the society of those who have been blessed by the friendship of Jesus and want to offer that blessing to others. Indeed, the proper name of the Quakers is the Society of Friends. We are friends of each other in the company of the Best Friend. (So why do we fall out so much?)

What could we do differently?

- We could make sure that friendship features as a significant part of our social existence; that is, that we value and nurture our friend-ships. Some people are naturally gifted in this and I've been privileged to have had a number of people who haven't been put off by my incompetence at sustaining contact. They have loved me enough to keep in contact and refresh the friendship at regular intervals. But if we aren't naturally gifted in this way we could at least practise the skills of friendship. Notes, emails, texts and phone calls are all easily achieved if meetings are infrequent. It's worth going out of our way to maintain friendships, not only to save ourselves from eventually slipping into isolation but also because it's part of the divine ecology: 'It is not good for the man to be alone.'

- The church we belong to is not primarily an institution, although it inevitably has many institutional characteristics. First of all it's a network of friends, friends of each other and friends of God. One of the early Fathers of the Church, Gregory of Nyssa, said at the end of his life: 'The most important thing is to be God's friend.' And to be God's friends together can be one of the most exhilarating and exciting experiences life has to offer. Perhaps we can try and see our own church in that way and work towards achieving it. We can help to re-vision the church as the place where Jesus is at the centre, living in his friends and empowering them to live his abundant life for each other and for the community around. Then anything is possible.

- It's important that in the church we 'think single'. So much of church life is orientated either towards the elderly who make up the present church or the younger families we hope will become the future church. But large numbers of regular churchgoers are single, whether they are young singles, widows, widowers, divorcees, students, migrants, single parents or those coming to church unsupported by a partner. There are many categories, but each person is a friend of God. Our church activities need to reflect this diverse make-up and not assume everyone is part of a 'traditional' happy family. This means care in the use of language, events that aren't predicated on family life, and the involvement of everyone in ministry. 'Think single.'

- There's special value in maintaining same-sex friends or groups of friends, even if we've become committed to a permanent partnership. Relationships aren't best reduced to a generic sameness. Men may well want to be able to talk sport; women may well want to set up book groups (no stereotyping here!). Retaining these friendships is both a personal responsibility but also something that the church can facilitate. Men's breakfasts, women's lunches, sports outings, health spa visits – all these can be sponsored by churches that recognize the importance of friendships and the particular point of single-gender groups. And if these don't exist in your church, why not start them? Friendships with the opposite sex are also important, giving us the widest opportunity for natural, holistic, complementary relationships, across the spectrum of humankind. Everyone is a potential gift to us. Remember too the value of inter-generational friendships. If families are widely scattered, it can be a real enrichment to adopt a granny or a young person to broaden the range of everyone's experience and affection.

They said this

Don't walk behind me; I may not lead. Don't walk in front of me; I may not follow. Just walk beside me and be my friend.

(Albert Camus)[3]

When we honestly ask ourselves which person in our lives means the most to us, we often find that it is those who, instead of giving advice, solutions, or cures, have chosen rather to share our pain and touch our wounds with a warm and tender hand. The friend who can be silent with us in a moment of despair or confusion, who can stay with us in an hour of grief and bereavement, who can tolerate not knowing, not curing, not healing and face with us the reality of our powerlessness, that is a friend who cares.   (Henri Nouwen)[4]

I think if I've learned anything about friendship, it's to hang in, stay connected, fight for them, and let them fight for you. Don't walk away, don't be distracted, don't be too busy or tired, don't take them for granted. Friends are part of the glue that holds life and faith together. Powerful stuff.   (Jon Katz, writer)[5]

Taking it further

Anchor passage: John 15.12–17
Read once, take a full two minutes to reflect, then read it again.

To think about

Opener: Have everyone talk for a while to the group about a special friend and why that person has meant so much to them.

- 'To lay down one's life for one's friends' is something of a cliché, but when have you come closest to seeing it done and understanding what it means?
- 'You are my friends if you do what I command you' (v. 14). There are obviously some differences between this friendship and our human friendships. What are they?
- 'You did not choose me but I chose you' (v. 16). Has that been your experience?
- 'There's often considerable confusion about how male and female are to relate if not as a couple.' Do we have a problem here? And if so, how should we handle these relationships?
- How could your church 'think single' more effectively?

Prayer: Place a cross or candle in the middle with a bowl in front. Give each person four slips of paper and ask them to write the name of a special friend on each one. Then give the group three or four minutes in which to give thanks and pray for each friend, putting the slip of paper in the bowl. Rounding up prayer to finish.

15

Building community

It was the Queen's Diamond Jubilee and it was raining. Our street party had to move indoors to a local school. Over 200 people turned up, dripping from the unwelcome weather but bearing gifts – mountains of sandwiches, cakes, paper cups, bottles of cloudy lemonade. These were my neighbours and I hardly knew any of them. We live in our domestic fortresses and drive past each other every morning to the station or on the school run, without recognition or a smile. But now I think it will be different. We've met, talked, laughed at the rain; we've learnt names and interests and recent experiences (nothing too heavy yet). We've begun to build community.

One of the gifts the Church has to offer society is its experience of building community. We've been doing it for centuries so we know a thing or two. Politicians and pundits bemoan our social fragmentation and cast around for cures; the Church modestly gets on with it. Building community is part of our discipleship – living in God's world, in God's way, with God's help.

What's the problem?

We live in an atomized society where everyone gets on with constructing their own 'this-must-fit-me-precisely' world. This involves smoothing out the rough edges and creating a bubble of work, leisure pursuits and friendships in which we feel comfortable. It also means keeping ourselves to ourselves and eliminating from our bubble the people we don't much like. Since the 1970s there has been a noticeable decline in participation in political parties, trade unions, civic groups, church life and the like. Repeatedly, surveys show younger people to be less interested in public life and more interested in personal relationships and private lives. This 'turn to the self' has probably become more marked because it has become more possible: previous generations more obviously needed each other for support and for home-made entertainment. In north Oxford we can get on without each other.

At another level, in the West we are the prisoners of rationalism: 'I think, therefore I am.' In Africa they prefer 'I am, because we belong.' The individualism of the West asserts our unique identity, but sadly it nearly always seems to do so at the expense of others. We define ourselves over against others rather than as part of the whole. This can be seen writ large when a dominant group wants to establish its own identity by marking out and naming an enemy. The result has been seen in Hitler's concentration camps, Stalin's gulags, Maoist re-education camps, Pinochet's interrogation rooms, Pol Pot's death camps, Rwandan Hutu death squads, Bosnian-Serb and Syrian militia groups and so on. The process is always the same: define yourself, identify an enemy, eliminate the other. The opposite process is to build community.

How could we think about this?

Christians can root their concern with community right back in the nature of God. To put it at its most basic, God is community, a free and interactive fellowship of Father, Son and Holy Spirit. It's in the loving interplay of the Trinity that we see the model of creative inter-dependence that we seek to replicate in God's world. And it's from that mutual delight that the Church receives its energy to build community, both in its own life and in that of the world around. If you have diffi-culty getting your head round the idea of the Trinity, read *The Shack* for a quirky picture that takes the Trinity out of the dusty theological cupboard and fires the imagination with unexpected images.[1]

Jesus clearly decided that the way to approach his glorious and dangerous task was to gather and nurture a small community of young people who would be his core team of kingdom-builders. If he hoped that they would 'get it' in his lifetime, he was badly let down. But he knew the raw material he was taking on; the seeds were being sown. If ever we feel disappointed with our church community, think of this motley band of brothers and the difficulties Jesus had with, among others, a hot-head, two status seekers, a fraudster, a terrorist, a doubter and a traitor. Perhaps our local fellowship isn't so bad after all. But Jesus knew that he had to build a community, and that when everything fell into place, suitably empowered, this community was the way to change the world.

At first sight, when reading Acts 2 it appears that the disciples did indeed 'get it'. The earliest days were idyllic. They shared possessions, looked after the needy, ate together, prayed together and found people joining them in enviable numbers (Acts 2.42–47). Isn't that what they were meant to be doing? Well, no, actually. They had been a travelling, missionary community gathered around Jesus, and now they had become a static community locked into Jerusalem. It took the killing of Stephen and the resulting persecution to scatter the disciples, old and new, and help them recover their original mandate to be a missionary community on the move. There's an important principle here: community happens when you're not looking, when you're doing something else. If the disciples had stayed in Jerusalem 'having the goodwill of all the people' (v. 47), the Church would eventually have faded away and been a footnote in religious history. I'll return to the importance of this principle later.

Paul was the Church's first theologian and he did his theology on the run. But he realized early on that what the death and resurrection of Jesus had done was no less than to inaugurate a new creation under their noses. This was a world order in which all barriers were broken down and a new community had come into being 'in Christ'. 'In Christ' everything looked different, and indeed it was different. 'If anyone is in Christ, there is a new creation: everything old has passed away; see, everything has become new!' (2 Corinthians 5.17). The old hierarchies and barriers had collapsed: 'There is no longer Jew or Greek, there serving the wider community that the special belonging of *communitas* occurs by happy accident. Have you noticed how energized people are by going with a group on short-term service in Africa or putting on a theatrical performance or playing in an orchestra or taking part in a sports team? Are Christians fired with the same passion by being members of their churches? Only, I suggest, when the church is focused beyond itself, when it's missional.

- This is where our commitment to the local community ties in naturally with commitment to the church community. We are at our best in the church when we are working actively for the flourishing of the community around us. I once encountered a town where the churches got together for a weekend every year to put on 'Operation Inasmuch'. They were inspired by the teaching of Matthew 25 where Jesus says that 'inasmuch' as his listeners cared for others they were caring for him. So the churches offered the community an enormous range of support and help. They would cut hedges, clean out ponds, decorate rooms, clear attics, look after children, wash windows, take the housebound out for the day – anything they could reasonably do to help others. The result was a sense of anticipation, togetherness and achievement, both for the churches and for the wider community. Relationships were built, barriers were broken down, community was being shaped in the town and *communitas* in the churches. But note – this service was being done without ulterior motive. We need to serve the community around *for its own sake* and not to go fishing for souls. Any by-product like that is God's business.

- What the church at its best can demonstrate is the inclusiveness of a good community. Everyone is valued not for their wealth, status or gifts but because they are a child of God and a citizen of the new creation of Jesus. Where else in society do you get such a wonderful mix of unlikely friends? Civic groups are usually self-limiting and like attracts like. In churches, age, background, education, employment, colour, gender, sexuality and all the other variables shouldn't matter, for we are 'all one in Christ Jesus'. Yes, we sometimes get it horribly wrong, but usually we get it wonderfully right. It would be good to

- Do you expect the church to have 'the goodwill of all the people' (v. 47)? If not, why not?
- What difference is your church making to the local community? How could it make more impact?
- How can we balance the use of a finite amount of energy between building up the fellowship in faith and serving the community around?

Prayer: With a map before you, identify the main centres of life and activity in your area or parish (schools, town hall, commercial life, leisure centre, village hall and so on). Place a night light on the map where that activity is going on, and pray for the flourishing of that place and the people involved there.

16

Sharing faith

———•◆•———

It was excruciating. I was a young Christian and had been told that I had to share my faith, so I invited a hapless victim for lunch and then tried clumsily to turn the conversation to Christianity at any available opening. The meal went on and I became ever more panicky as I failed to make any connection. At the end of lunch I felt crushed with embarrassment and my victim probably wondered what it had all been about. We never had lunch together again.

This is not what I mean when I write that sharing our faith is part of living faithfully. On the other hand, there is a central dynamic in the Christian faith that is to do with sharing the good news of Jesus, and if we slip into the kingdom through the door that says 'Nothing to declare' we're selling Jesus short.

What's the problem?

The kingdom of God is a society transformed by love, justice and joy. Our task is to help transform human society so that it overlaps as far as possible with the life of the kingdom, of which Jesus spoke so much. If this is to happen we need people to do it, so the more people who sign up to the task, the more impact we can make. It isn't a matter of trying to fill pews for its own sake; it's a matter of filling our world with the love of God. People who go to church often think the task is to get other people to go to church, but that's the mentality of a club, not a church.

British Christians are so reticent about their faith. Perhaps we forget that someone, sometime, somehow, helped us take faith seriously, and if we don't do that for the next generation then we die out. Maybe we're scared of sharing our faith with others because it's too personal or too controversial or we feel too unprepared for honest exchanges about belief in God. We're not sure we have answers to the old chestnuts (suffering, science, other faiths) and certainly not to the new chestnuts (Dawkins, multiverses, violent religion). So it's easier to keep smiling and carry on.

At the Lambeth Conference of Anglican bishops from around the world in 2008, Brian McLaren showed us a picture of a road bridge in Honduras after a hurricane. There were no longer any roads leading up to the bridge, and the river that the bridge used to cross had changed its course and gone elsewhere. The result was a bridge that no longer did anything of any value. Brian used this as a metaphor for a church from which society has moved away, but our structures, our ways of thinking and our practices of faith have remained stuck in realities now passed.

> **Things you can say to kill off evangelism before it's started**
>
> 'I suppose we ought to do something about it . . .'
> 'We're still waiting for the information from the diocese . . .'
> 'The Bishop is terribly keen . . .'
> 'Faith is a very personal matter for Anglicans . . .'
> 'It might solve our financial problems . . .'
> 'Our vicar isn't very good at this sort of thing . . .'
> 'We need to get the church roof sorted first . . .'
> 'But we're doing evangelism all the time . . .'

How could we think about this?

What motivates me to want to share my faith is found in a basic question: how could I not want to share the best thing I've ever found? It happens with a book I've just read, a film I've just seen, a holiday destination I've just enjoyed; how much more with a faith that's given coherence and direction to my entire life? On the other hand, our reticence might cause us to ask just how important our faith really is to us . . .

How do we pick up anything new? It's nearly always because someone was enthusiastic enough to tell us about it. People rarely become Christians because of a search for propositional truth; it usually happens because friends demonstrate by the way they live that there's something worth exploring. Someone said: 'I didn't agree with his arguments, but I couldn't disagree with his life.'

It's important to remember that Jesus never invited people to come to church (synagogue) or say a prayer of commitment. St Peter didn't share the Four Spiritual Laws with anyone or invite them to receive Christ as their personal Saviour. Jesus met people on their territory, used their language and spoke of things that mattered to them. Isn't that a good set of principles for us too? Jesus simply left lots of calling cards that said: 'The kingdom of God is here. (Did you notice?)' Our sharing of faith needs to be less of a sales pitch or an argument or a demand and more of a conversation, a friendship, an invitation, an opportunity, an exploration. We're inviting people to take part in an adventure. Certainly you have to sign up to start the journey, but it's an open road all the way into the kingdom.

We need to believe that God is always there before us. There's no situation where we're dragging God in or bringing someone to his notice of whom he's not been aware. God is always present, seeking to turn hearts to love and trust. We simply come in long afterwards and try to catch up with what God is doing. There are never only two of us in a conversation.

What could we do differently?

The liquid gold of the gospel has to be poured into the new moulds of today. That means attending to specific aspects of the way people live, think and behave in our culture. For example:

- *Relationships* Faith is best shared in natural conversations. Imagine you've prepared a special dish for a dinner party. You could be so confident in the popularity of the recipe that you have it printed out beforehand and placed beneath each plate. You could then ask everyone to read out the recipe before they leave the table. Alternatively, you could simply all enjoy the dish and then if anyone says 'That was lovely; could I have the recipe?' you can then say you'll give them a copy when they leave. One approach is the classic hard sell; the other is the gracious sharing of good things with friends. But food is often a great way of opening up conversation; hence the popularity of men's and women's breakfasts, meals at Alpha courses, fun barbecues and so on. The important principle is about making a friend and being a friend before introducing that person to a special Friend. How are meals used in your church as openings for the sharing of faith?

☆ *When Max Warren was General Secretary of what was then the Church Missionary Society he was invited to an African village to celebrate the anniversary of the opening of the church. The building was packed with 600 people. After a marvellous service Max Warren asked how the church had started. He was told that it all began when two women from a neighbouring village came to do their washing in the market place, and as they did so, they just chatted about Jesus.*

• *Process* Research regularly shows that by far the majority of people (over 70 per cent) come to faith as a process that starts with a friendly invitation to come along to an event. Very few people walk in off the streets and get converted on the spot, or even come to faith as a result of a week's mission. Most people meet Christ on the road to Emmaus rather than the road to Damascus. They meet Christ in others and talk on the way, rather than being flung from their high horse by a blinding light. The average length of time the journey takes has been found to be around four to five years if people are starting from right outside the world of faith. So it's important to find places that gently encourage that process rather than force it. The ancient wisdom of the Catechumenate[1] has much to commend it, offering as it does milestones on the journey into faith. Different courses can help the journey along – Alpha, Emmaus,

Christianity Explored, Start-CPAS (see websites through a search engine), and so can open-ended groups such as one we ran in the church I served called No Holds Barred, because that was exactly the nature of the discussion. There were no right or wrong answers; nothing was off-limits. Every church needs neutral spaces where Christianity can be explored, not sold. Does your church have such a space?

- *Community* A church that simply lives the gospel, not self-consciously but graciously and generously, is always going to be the most powerful witness to the truth and value of the faith that lies at its core. In the early church you get the feeling that evangelism happened naturally, spontaneously, continuously, contagiously, like light issuing from the sun. What I long for in our churches is that the spiritual temperature of our communities rises to boiling point; then renewal and evangelism happens effortlessly. Occasionally you meet such a community and are delighted in it, but we need always to remember that it will fall at some point because that's the nature of human communities. Yet even in the falling, truly Christian communities will exhibit something of the character of Christ, and that itself can be converting. Constant outward success can never be the distinctive characteristic of those who follow a man who was crucified. But even in the dying, a new world was being born. Is your church a 'community of grace'? And if not, what would help it on the journey?
- *Service* A church that lives to itself will die to itself. If our goal is the transformation of all life under God then we exist for the flourishing of others, not for the religious entertainment of ourselves. Service comes at a cost, but it's precisely that cost, paid millions of times every day by Christians all over the world, that accounts for the phenomenal growth of the Church worldwide. It's when we engage seriously with the real experience of the community around us that the community around us takes us seriously. I know a church where there are 170 children and young people in their Saturday morning football club. Christianity isn't pushed at anyone, but they say a prayer in the centre circle before they start their games. Street Pastors and detached youth work programmes are widely supported by the police as major factors in keeping peace in

our communities. I know one such youth work scheme that resulted in an 80 per cent reduction in summer crime rates. Food banks are bringing essential relief to increasing numbers of hard-pressed families; scores of such banks have been set up in recent years by churches working together. Holiday clubs, lunch clubs, driving schemes, community shops, credit unions – these are the visible signs of a serving church, modelling these actions on a man who said he had come not to be served but to serve (Mark 10.45). And always the church is there to handle competently and carefully the celebrations, sorrows and transitions of families and communities. Service is love in full colour. It heightens curiosity and prepares the ground for deeper questions. How seriously does our church – or do we – demonstrate that selfless service?

* *Worship* Sunday – and increasingly weekday – services are still the shop window of our faith, so it matters that we take worship seriously and don't just turn the handle week after week. Every act of worship is potentially a converting experience for someone. When I was a vicar and I saw a new couple in church, I could never avoid seeing the rest of the service through their eyes. What would they be making of this, of this, of this? Variety, quality, participation and many other factors need to be constantly in view as worship is prepared. God is worthy of the very best we can create and the very best that we can offer, even if we are sitting in the pew. We can then have greater confidence when we invite neighbours to join us on Back to Church Sunday.[2] But why only on that Sunday?

They said this

We Christians have done 1001 things that Jesus never commanded us to do, but we have failed in the two new commands that he gave the Church. We have failed to 'love one another', and we have failed to 'preach the gospel to every nation'. (Neil Rowe)

Aiden was Bishop of Lindisfarne (died 651) and when he met people he would ask: 'Do you love God?' If they said yes he would say, 'Then love him more.' If they said no he would say, 'Then can I tell you about Jesus?'

Taking it further

Anchor passage: John 3.1–16 (everyone should have their own copy of the text)
Explain that when the passage is read out everyone will be asked to identify one word or phrase that strikes them. Two minutes' silence will be given, and then these words or phrases will be shared, without any explanation. Then the passage will be read again, with a further two minutes for reflection, after which everyone will be asked to say why they chose their phrase and what it means to them. Further discussion may follow. Having explained the process, try it out.

- How did you find a 'living' faith? Give everyone a chance, but don't embarrass any seekers.
- How do you hear that phrase about being 'born again' ('born from above') in v. 7? Does it alarm you or is it spot on?
- Do Christians 'speak of what we know and testify to what we have seen' (v. 11), or do we keep quiet? What experiences have encouraged us or scared us off?
- If we love sharing good things, and evangelism is sharing the best thing we know, why do we find it so difficult and what would make it easier?
- Does v. 16 encapsulate what you believe is the heart of the gospel or is there another verse or phrase that you prefer?

Prayer: Recall and name in the group the people who brought the good news to you; that is, those who helped you to find a faith that lasted. Write down their names and place these in a bowl of thanksgiving. The leader offers thanks for these good people. Then think of those to whom you would like to bring the good news – family, friends, neighbours. Write down their names, and as each puts the names into another bowl, pause to pray for those people. Take the pieces of paper home (either your own or another's) and use them as a spur to pray.

PART 5

Facing the future

———◆•◆•◆———

We live in an exciting and dangerous world. The speed of change is getting ever faster; the planet is looking more vulnerable than we ever imagined; the digital world has extended our reach phenomenally. And in this context, religion has proved to be a force for great good and considerable evil. What does living faithfully mean in this new world? What do Christians bring to the debates and dilemmas of our day? And how do we face our own ultimate destiny?

17

Handling future shock

There was a period of my life when I remember being profoundly anxious for the future of my family and of the world. It was the time leading up to 1984, when the possibility of a nuclear holocaust seemed a real possibility, when the stakes were very high indeed and the debate on how to lower the nuclear temperature was deeply serious. I looked into the night sky and wondered how we would survive a nuclear winter and what, if anything, I could do to protect my family.

We came through. But just before the millennium a speechwriter for Presidents Reagan and Bush Sr wrote this:

Something's up. And deep down, where the body meets the soul, we are fearful. We fear, down so deep it hasn't even risen to the point of articulation, that with all our comforts and amusements, with all our toys and bells and whistles, we wonder if what we have is a first class state room on the *Titanic*. Everything's wonderful, but a world is ending and we sense it. I don't mean 'Uh-oh, there's a depression coming.' I mean: We live in a world with three billion men and hundreds of thousands of nuclear bombs, missiles, warheads; it's a world of extraordinary germs that can be harnessed and used to do the same. Three billion men, and it takes only half a dozen bright and evil ones to harness and deploy. What are the odds it will happen? Put it another way: what are the odds it will not? Low. Non-existent, I think.[1]

What's the problem?

The quote above makes it rather clear. We're facing changes in our technological capability that make the future safety of our fragile little planet extremely precarious. The distinguished cosmologist Professor Martin Rees wrote: 'I think the odds are no better than fifty–fifty that our present civilisation on Earth will survive to the end of the present century without a serious setback.'[2] He names biological superweapons, nuclear terrorism, virus epidemic attacks, laboratory errors, renegade nuclear states, nanotechnology that goes rampant, catastrophic climate change, population growth that exhausts the world and so on. The list is fearful. If, instead of flying aircraft into the Twin Towers, the 9/11 terrorists had caused nuclear explosions using two lumps of enriched uranium no larger than grapefruits, hundreds of thousands of people would have been killed and the resultant panic would have been overwhelming. Because the techniques for making biological weapons will soon become dispersed worldwide among hospital labs, agricultural research institutes and elsewhere, there will be tens of thousands of people who could acquire the capability to disseminate weapons that could cause regional or even worldwide epidemics. Dr Strangelove has arrived.

We are encountering the future faster than we can assimilate it. The phenomenon is called 'future shock'.[3] We're caught in a tidal wave of change that gives us no chance to adjust practically, emotionally or ethically. In a robotic world, what duty of care will we have to robots that have an 'intelligence' greater than ours? With brain implants, will we be able to 'plug in' extra memory, or learn for exams by direct input into the brain? With a world population of nine billion, if the only way for the race to survive is to limit people to subsisting on a rice-based diet, travelling very little and finding entertainment in virtual reality, is that an acceptable price to pay? So many questions; so little time to work them out.

We need perhaps to remember that there's always a 'scare you to death' industry searching for new prey. One of the most terrifying scenarios is of experiments with the forces that govern particle physics in places like CERN in Geneva. It's been suggested that crashing together an atom of gold and an atom of lead could result in an unprecedented implosion that could have three possible outcomes. First, there could be a black hole into which we would all disappear. Second, quarks might assemble into a 'stanglet' that makes the oceans solid. Third, a transition could occur that could rip the fabric of space itself and destroy all atoms in our galaxy. You will be glad to know that such an eventuality is almost completely impossible (though what does 'almost completely' mean?). But humankind is fascinated by doomsday scenarios and there are many who will take advantage of that propensity.

How could we think about all this?

In the first place, Christians will want to assert that the largest problems need the largest resources brought to them, and that means the Originator and Sustainer of all that exists, otherwise known as God. Facing human problems with human resources is only part of the answer. We need to be available to the divine energy and wisdom that infuses all life, and so to align ourselves with the good grain of the universe. The ancient wisdom of the world's great faiths has been carved out of the hard rocks of human experience and divine revelation. Prayer and sanctified intelligence are not the least of our resources when facing the world's seemingly overwhelming issues.

Christianity offers a unique gift to a bewildered world in the way it embraces a complete scale of past, present and future. Contemporary Western culture tries to live in a perennial present, grabbing whatever pleases us and using whatever comes to hand. It was noticeable that in the Millennium Dome in London we chose to present ourselves as living in a frenzy of superficial gizmos rather than as having been shaped by a deep, soul-making history. Everything was bright and shiny – and ephemeral. A culture that has no past is condemned to perpetual new beginnings and repeated mistakes. The Christian faith on the other hand is deeply rooted in a story of divine–human interaction that has given the world some of its most important beliefs, values, wisdoms and learnings, whether they be about living together in community, preserving personal dignity and human rights, creating democratic structures and legal systems or inspiring human creativity in science and the arts. We are what we have come from.

Christianity also offers society a future hope by emphasizing that history has a trajectory that is both of and not of this world. This eschatological perspective provides a context for our perplexities and struggles. We're not alone, swimming further and further out into the darkness. We're driving forward to a future that is unknown but secure, held in the hands of a God of infinite grace and goodness. A friend of mine used to say that, because of the reliability of God, 'everything is cosmically OK', a modern translation of Julian of Norwich's famous affirmation that 'All shall be well, and all shall be well, and all manner of things shall be well.'[4] If we have that confidence then we're released from the paralysis that grips so many in society when faced with overwhelming problems. Love frees us to work for change. Redemption is always a possibility for those who have lived with Jesus through Good Friday and seen him walk free of a grave on Easter morning. 'Have courage. Love has all eternity to achieve its purposes. And it will.'[5]

At the same time as having this rootedness in the past and confidence in the future, Christian disciples are aware that the present is the only time we have in which to live. 'There are three realities in the mind,' said St Augustine. 'The present of past things is memory, the present of present things is attention, and the present of future things is expectation.'[6] So the present is all we have, and it's in the eternal present that we have to make moral choices, to live justly, to love mercy and to walk humbly with our God. Christians are therefore offering society a scale of reality that embraces an entire range from past, through present, to future. A Christian understanding of life gives wraparound assurance of the significance of what we say and do, and of the One who holds it together.

☆ *In the winter of 1941, the composer Olivier Messiaen was one of a group of prisoners of war in Stalag 8A in Silesia. He had read the*

Gospels and the book of Revelation and had come to believe that Jesus would return. He knew that this hope created meaning for the suffering people around him. In their appalling conditions he understood that hope for tomorrow was essential for life today. He looked around the concentration camp and managed to gather together four instruments: a cello with a missing string, a battered violin, an old clarinet and a piano with stuck-together keys. For this unusual combination of broken instruments, he wrote one of the greatest pieces of music of the twentieth century, and Messiaen called it, 'Quartet for the End of Time'. When it was played to 5,000 prisoners of war in that freezing place in Silesia, the audience listened with rapt attention. Messiaen records, 'The cold was excruciating, the Stalag buried under snow, the four performers played on broken-down instruments, but never have I had an audience who listened with such rapt attention and comprehension.'[7] God can use us as agents of hope in a dangerous world.

What could we do differently?

- We could live today as citizens of the world as we would like it to become. This means planting a flag in the future and believing that the world could be different. The question we need to ask is, 'What will be left when we've left?' The Christian hope is not a vague, fluffy optimism that things will get better. Hope is an action, a clear-eyed engagement with the problems we face in the light of confidence in a loving and purposeful God. It matters, therefore, whether we engage with the political process, get involved with local and national charities, speak up for asylum seekers, support moves to lower carbon consumption, help children to believe in their potential to achieve and so on. The question to ask ourselves is whether we are making a difference. Is the light of the kingdom filtering in anywhere because of what we're doing? It absolutely doesn't have to be dramatic (most people's lives aren't at all dramatic), but Christians are people with a goal. Jesus encouraged us in parable after parable to live towards

God's future. He opened the door of the kingdom, but we have to walk through. That's where we belong.

- We can insist on being people of hope. The media constantly pump bad news at us. Sometimes we're surprised the world has lasted another day, so many are the crises breaking over our vulnerable planet. But the Christian emphasis on hope suggests that we move from saying 'Who do we blame for the past?' to 'How shall we create the future?' We are privileged to live in two worlds at once – the world of present problems and the world of future hope. The kingdoms of this world have a pall of gloom lying over them; the kingdom of God is a constant encouragement that it will not always be so. 'Your kingdom come *on earth*,' we pray. The new creation is not for some saccharine afterlife, but for now and for the future, for this world and the next. Be a person of irresistible hope.

- We can try always to engage Christianly with the people and situations we encounter in the particular arena of life we occupy. All of us are faced with the shock of the future but, for each of us, we are the only person who can respond to that challenge in the particular place we are set, with the particular decisions and the particular pressures we face. This is true whether we are accountants, teaching assistants, software engineers, bank personnel, shop workers, clergy, professional athletes (I'm writing this during the Olympics) or whoever. What are the resources we have for living Christianly? We always have *the life of Jesus*, overflowing with wisdom and material for reflection. We have the gifts of *theology* (I hope we all read Christian books that push us further – only 10 per cent of Christians do). Our *praying and waiting on God* are vital sources of strength. Asking '*What would Jesus do?*' is no sentimental sticking plaster, either. *Christian instinct* is a profound source of wisdom if we've been shaped by the mind of Christ over the years. The resources we have are many. Living faithfully requires that we use them.

- It should be obvious from the scale of the problems we have identified that the answers have to be political, scientific and moral.

In every arena of human activity there are Christians seeking to do the right thing by the Lord they follow. There are top-flight and believing scientists; there are politicians driven by high ideals and religious motivation; there are civil servants, designers and entrepreneurs who want to make a difference. They have crucial roles in rescuing the earth. And those of us who are not placed in such responsibilities can still unleash the great resource of prayer for those on the front line. We can do no less, but we can also do no more.

They said this

Two views from the same man (note the dates):

Can we doubt that presently our race will more than realise our boldest imaginations, that it will achieve unity and peace, and that our children will live in a world more splendid and lovely than any garden or palace that we know, going on from strength to strength in an ever-widening circle of achievement? What man has done, the little triumphs of his present state, form but the prelude to the things than man has yet to do.

(H. G. Wells, *A Short History of the World*, 1937)

The cold-blooded massacres of the defenceless, the return of deliberate and organised torture, mental torture and fear to a world from which such things seemed well nigh banished – has come near to breaking my spirit altogether. 'Homo sapiens' as he has been pleased to call himself, is played out.

(H. G. Wells, *Mind at the End of its Tether*, 1946)

The world hangs on a thin thread and that thread is the psyche of man. It is not the reality of the hydrogen bomb we must fear, but what man does with it . . . As never before, the world hangs on the psyche of man.

(Carl Jung)

I hope that when insects take over the world, they will remember
with gratitude how we took them along on all our picnics.

(Bill Vaughan)

Taking it further

Anchor passage: Revelation 21.1–7
Read once, take a full two minutes to reflect, then read it again.

To think about
Opener: On a scale of 1–10, how much do you agree with Martin Rees
on the 50–50 chance of the world surviving to the end of the century
without a serious setback? And why?

* What range of responses do you have to the picture in Revelation
  21?
* Does the image of a new heaven and a new earth suggest to you
  continuity or discontinuity from the first heaven and the first earth
  (v. 1)?
* Tears, death, mourning, crying and pain will disappear (v. 4). But
  aren't they essential to our nature as free men and women? So how
  do we envisage heaven?
* Is there anything we personally, or we as a church, can do to contribute to some minimizing of risk in our dangerous world?

Prayer: Take out the map you used for 'Making peace' (Chapter 10) and
place night lights on it while you pray together for places of special
anxiety. For more general fears and hopes, place a candle in the oceans
(that 'the earth may be filled with the glory of God as the waters cover
the sea').

18

Loving the planet

———◆———

In the film *Titanic*, the Chief Engineer comes to see the Captain at a very smart table and tells him the ship has hit an iceberg, the damage isn't repairable and they'll sink in a fairly short time. The idea is so far fetched the people at the table simply laugh and carry on as if nothing has happened. Is that too dramatic a way of representing our current attitude to what's happening to our planet because of climate change and environmental damage? Many scientists and pundits are telling us there's a fierce urgency about this issue. Young people seem to have got the message more than their elders – they see it as a new moral imperative. Unfortunately it's their elders who are in charge of the ship.

What's the problem?

At its most basic, this precious little planet is getting exhausted. It has been estimated that by 2030 we'll need the resources of two earths to keep up with the demands we make on it.[1] An area of rainforest the size of a football pitch is cut down every four seconds.[2] Ninety per cent of our edible fish stock has disappeared and yet we still build larger fishing fleets. Every day we're taking from the earth's aquifers 400 million tons of water more than is being replaced by rain. (If that quantity of water were carried in water trucks it would need 25 million of them – every day!)[3] A population of seven billion people asking for more and more of the world's finite resources is unsustainable. UN Secretary General Ban Ki-moon spoke of the world's current economic model as a 'global suicide pact'.[4]

Global warming is highly dangerous when the earth has such a thin skin. This fragile biosphere is so incredibly complex that it's highly dangerous to interfere with its delicate balance. It's almost certain that by the late 2030s the average world temperature will have risen by at least two degrees over the baseline that's existed since civilization began. It may even climb to four degrees or more over that baseline. The climate may then be sliding into a new state that is hostile to human beings, particularly in certain vulnerable areas. It may be very nice for Scotland to have the climate of Cornwall, but in northern Africa life will be unsustainable and macro-migration will be the norm, with Europe the main target.

Futurologist James Martin wrote:

> If we continue as now seems likely, a crunch is coming – in fact three crunches – our global footprint greatly exceeding what the Earth can support, climate destabilisation becoming severe, and fresh water becoming insufficient to feed the Earth's large population. These crunches will not, by themselves, destroy humanity but they will cause a Darwinian situation; when the going gets tough there will be survival of the fittest. By mid-century, the Earth could be like a lifeboat that's too small to save everyone.[5]

Who will survive? China has been preparing. The USA is powerful and resourceful. Europe has a question mark over it. Japan will struggle. Russia will muddle through because of its scale. So who will end up paying the price?

As usual, it's the poorest who will end up paying our bills. Those in third class on the *Titanic* found the gates on to the deck were locked; when they got out, there was no room left on the lifeboats. Rising temperatures, rising sea levels, rising prices, famine, mass migration, radicalized politics, water wars and more – all of this will assault the poorest countries. Those travelling in first class may well find that they're being invaded by steerage, and the battles could be fierce.

There are four basic laws of ecology:

1 Everything is connected to everything else. When humans interfere with any part of the environment, they're likely to upset some other part.
2 Everything must go somewhere. Science says matter can be changed, but it can neither be created nor destroyed.
3 Nature knows best. Nature's ecological principles work, and human beings should always copy them.
4 There's no such thing as a free lunch. To live takes energy, and you can never get out of a natural system as much energy as goes in.[6]

Is God saying something?

How could we think about this?

Christian disciples have got to protest at this misuse of creation. We start from the position of valuing a world that is intrinsically good. By verse 3 of the first chapter of Genesis we are being told: 'God saw that the light was good', and that formula of the goodness of creation is repeated four more times before humanity even comes on the scene. The natural world is wonderful in the sight of God, and to be respected and enjoyed by humankind *just for itself*. We have sometimes got into trouble over the phrase 'have dominion' in verse 28, as if that has encouraged the plundering of this glorious creation. The word 'dominion' takes us back to the Latin *dominus*, meaning 'lord of the house' (*domus*). Men and women are being told to be like God, and to love and care for the land as God does. Thus the command is not exploitative but protective. Moreover, humans are created last in the Genesis scheme of things and are therefore naturally dependent on the animals and plants that have gone before. Humanity and the rest of creation are part of the same fabric, and the attitude of men and women needs to be one of humility and respect towards our common home.

There are a number of ways in which the proper relationship of human beings and the natural world can be described. All of them emphasize mutuality. The relationship may be of *stewardship*, with men and women caring for the welfare and flourishing of creation. Or it could be a relationship of *covenant*, with human beings covenanting with creation to seek mutual benefit. Or the relationship could be *redemptive*, with humanity charged with redeeming those parts of the natural order that have suffered degradation through what we poetically call the Fall. A fourth way of describing the relationship is *sacramental*, with the natural world being an outward and visible sign of the presence and goodness of God. All these descriptions speak of the interdependence of humanity and the rest of creation. We have no right to exploit, and every responsibility to care.

Indeed, we can push the sacramental image a stage further. The Eucharist, or Holy Communion, offers the idea of 'reverent consumption' to our discussion. When Christians receive bread and wine sacramentally, they're not looking for quantity. There's no place for greed or selfishness at the Communion table, as Paul pointed out to the little church in Corinth when he heard that when they gathered for the Lord's Supper, some Christians were having a wonderful picnic with the wine flowing liberally, while others were going hungry (1 Corinthians 11.17–22). When we receive the life of Christ through bread and wine, we are bound to eat and drink reflectively and reverently. This is holy ground, as it is when we consume the gifts of the earth.

In 2007 the Environment Agency asked 25 leading environmentalists and scientists to list 50 things that could help to save the planet. Saving energy was top of the list, but second was leadership from faith communities. This is where again we bump into the issue of what it is that will move the heart of human beings sufficiently to overcome our innate tendency to short-termism and self-interest. Facts don't do that, arguments don't either, ideologies might, but religions almost certainly do. Something has to penetrate to the soul.

Living in tune with creation

☆ *A village in China was suffering from extreme drought. Every remedy had been tried and eventually as a last resort the villagers sent for a rainmaker from another district. The rainmaker arrived, sniffed the air in a disapproving manner and asked for a cottage on the outskirts of the village where he could be entirely alone. There he remained for three days. At the end of that period it rained buckets. A visitor was amazed and sought out the old man and asked him if he could really make it rain. The man said: 'I come from a province where everything is in order, where the people are in Tao. It rains when it should and the crops are sown and reaped at the right season. But here the people are not in Tao. I felt it as soon as I arrived. I was infected by it. It took me three days to find the Tao again. Then naturally it rained.'*

What could we do differently?

- We have to set our own house in order (literally) before we can engage with any wider activity. The actions we need to take to ensure we're reducing our domestic carbon footprint are familiar, though not always followed through. Insulation, turning down heating, only boiling the water we need, turning technology off standby, putting a brick in the cistern, turning off lights, collecting rainwater, recycling everything possible, changing to green electricity, using public trans-port – the detailed actions are small but cumulatively huge if we all take them seriously. If every household reduced its hot water use by 5 per cent, the saving in CO_2 would be equivalent to taking nearly 600,000 cars off the road. Turning a photocopier off overnight saves as much energy as would have produced 1,500 copies.[7] The gains produced by small actions are clearly significant.
- What we buy and what we throw out are important in themselves, and also as symbols of a greater commitment. We tend to replace furniture, white goods, technology, clothes and so on, not when they need chang-ing but when we're tired of them or feel they show us in a poor light compared with other people. The principle of reverent consumption applies again. 'Do we really need it?' is a question not asked often enough. Could we make do for another year or two? Could we borrow? We throw away enough waste in the United Kingdom to fill the Albert Hall

every two hours. (Think how many bags of waste would be needed just to fill up your living room from top to toe.) Recycling has become much more common in recent years, so that now 24 per cent of household waste is recycled in the UK, making us the eleventh best recycling nation in the European Union, though still highly dependent on landfill.

- We could volunteer to champion environmental issues and carbon reduction in our own church, working with others, conducting an audit, making recommendations, taking action. We might join in wider networks of environmental groups, of which there are now a bewildering number. I chaired a conference in Oxfordshire to try and encourage more concerted planning and action across over 50 organizations in just one county. The goodwill is there and the Church is welcome. After all, we are the largest voluntary organization in the country, with deep roots in every community in the land.

- It's important to let our voice be heard more widely. We all have an MP and a vote, and access to petitions and pressure groups. We can refuse to be browbeaten by climate-change sceptics, while not being closed-minded on detail. We can inform ourselves, encourage children to get engaged, talk up the issue whenever possible (without becoming a climate-change bore). But everything must be done in a spirit of loving enjoyment of the natural world and a sense of wonder at the astonishing diversity of creation. We have a book open on a table at home, each double page of which reveals a breathtaking photograph of some part of the natural world. We turn a page a day, and each time something in me gasps.

They said this

If we seek to maintain the consumer economy indefinitely, ecological forces will dismantle it savagely.   (Alan Durning)[8]

The world's media have become increasingly full of images of collapsing ice shelves, stranded polar bears, raging hurricanes, lands stricken by drought, fires sweeping across southern Australia and deserts spreading. The icecaps are melting in both the Arctic and

Antarctic. But all this is only an overture to trouble on a much grander scale. The runaway transformation of the Earth's climate may become the worst crisis of human history.   (James Martin)[9]

God saw everything that he had made, and indeed, it was very good . . . and he rested on the seventh day.   (Genesis 1.31—2.2)

Taking it further

Anchor passage: Genesis 1.24—2.3
Read once, take a full two minutes to reflect, then read it again.

To think about
Opener: In the last five years, how much have you changed your lifestyle in response to all the new information we've been getting about climate change and environmental damage?

- '. . . have dominion over the fish of the sea' (v. 28). Is it fair that Christians should take the blame for humankind's abuse of the environment?
- It seems that until the fourth day in Genesis 1, God had been separating out light and darkness, water above and below, sea and dry land – in order to make space in the fifth and sixth day for creatures and humans to populate it appropriately. Is the idea of 'making space' helpful in a Christian approach to the environment?
- God rested on the seventh day. What are the deeper implications of that for the way we live with the rest of creation in the twenty-first century?
- What is the commitment of your own church to these issues, and how could the church move on one or two steps further? What could you do personally?

Prayer: Put on a table or a tray things like: flowers, grass, stones, berries, fruit, a picture of the earth from space, a glass of water, bread and wine, a Bible. Ask what people would like to pray about after the discussion and given the suggestive objects on the table. Then invite open prayer or gather up the ideas and offer the prayer yourself.

19

Living in an online world

————•◦•————

I'm one of the in-between generation. I got my first heavyweight word processor in 1989 and must have sent my first emails in about 1996. When using computers I 'get it' just so far – and then I call my wife. The digital future has arrived with a confidence bordering on arrogance. The generation after us is so completely at home with computing and all its digital offspring that it already seems hard-wired into them. If we can't manage (I nearly wrote 'hack it') we'll be left behind. The new poverty is an inability to surf the online world.

What's the problem?

Adjusting to new technologies requires people to be comfortable with constant flux. Today's newest gadgets are on tomorrow's rubbish heap. 'There is far more processing power in a computer game console than was available to the Apollo astronauts when they landed on the moon.'[1] But for those more used to gradual rather than exponential change, the need for such relentless mental adjustment has the effect of overwhelming people. It's easy to get disheartened and left behind.

Social networking has experienced truly astonishing growth. Facebook users have grown in number from a standing start at the end of 2004 to one billion at the end of 2012. Every statistic is out of date before it's published, but let's try one or two: every five minutes one and a half million people log on to Facebook. Here's another: if Facebook were a country it would be the third most populous nation on earth. What's more difficult to evaluate are the consequences for human interaction and family relationships. As people increasingly relate to each other through social networking, does that have the effect of further atomizing society into self-sealed human units, or does it open up a much wider range of social contacts? Will young people relate to the rest of the world through a screen (TV, computer, mobile, tablet, video game) or will they be enriched beyond measure by all they can access through three or four touches or clicks?

A further issue of concern is the widespread misuse of the internet so that porn sites abound, together with sites on torture and terrorism, mass murder, suicide pacts, even cannibalism. Cyber bullying on social networking sites has led to deep unhappiness, anxiety, self-harm and suicide. Paedophile grooming and stalking has also marked the rise of such sites. And there seems to be no limit to the degree of self-revelation some young people will offer, sometimes to the detriment of their self-image and safety. It's a ruthless and lawless world out there.

It's no longer at the far reaches of the imagination that we reflect on the possibility of system failure on a massive scale or cyber terrorism in the hands of desperate extremists. Either cause could bring about the meltdown of essential services on a colossal scale, leaving humankind helpless. Our financial services are especially vulnerable. In New York, 73 per cent of share transactions are performed by computers, without human involvement, and on one single day, 6 May 2010, 19.1 billion shares were traded, a number greater than had been traded in the entire decade of the 1960s.[2] Statistically, this reliance on computer technology, even with all its fail-safes and back-ups, seems bound to go catastrophically wrong at some point. Nothing lasts forever. (Discuss.)

How could we think about this?

It's important not to start with a negative mindset as if all we see around us is change and decay. The advances of the digital age are stupendous and enable us to communicate, educate, inform, innovate, design and so on, in astonishing ways. Human creativity is a wonderful gift. It started in the poetry of Eden and will last until the great drama of the new creation. We all have a share in this creativity, whether we design software, paint, teach, cook, garden or give birth to children. Nothing can stop us being creative. Our creativity marks us out as being made in the image of a creative God.

On the other hand, humanity has a propensity to corrupt and an uncanny ability to turn good things bad. Knives can cut fruit from a tree or life from an enemy. Gas can heat food for a family or slaughter Jews in a concentration camp. Jet engines can fly us round the globe or power murderous rockets. The doctrine of original sin has been said to be the only verifiable doctrine of the Christian faith. Roughly translated that means: 'If we can mess it up, we will.' This seems inevitable because experience has shown that the heart of the human problem is the problem of the human heart. Christianity is not only splendidly full of hope, it's also courageously realistic.

When we survey the achievements of the digital world we have one general test we can always apply: 'How does this look in the presence of Jesus Christ?' When you put the person of Christ alongside what appears on the internet, some is wonderfully in tune with him and some badly out of tune. There are worlds to discover and enjoy and there are worlds that will drag us down to base level. The test is always Jesus Christ, as revealed in his life, death and new life, in his teaching and healing, in his affirmation and challenge. As a rule of thumb, Jesus Christ is our true north and we need to take all our compass readings off him.

Peter Graystone wrote in the *Church Times*:

☆ *In 2011, I woke up to the significance of social networking. On an August evening in my Croydon flat, watching the flames from buildings set alight by rioters, I knew that, as all the clergy were on holiday, I needed to take action. The next morning I used Twitter to send a message that I would open the church for those who wanted to pray for the town. I asked anyone in Croydon to retweet it. At 8 p.m. I opened the doors and put out a dozen chairs. Fifty people came in. Half of them were young people. They had used Facebook that morning to organise themselves to take brooms to the town centre.*[3]

What could we do differently?

- It follows from the above that Christians will want to take full advantage of the extraordinary benefits of being able to 'skype' our children in distant cities and survey the surface of Mars from the comfort of our computer desk. But we will want to use the internet and social media with a discerning eye, aware of the possible consequences. Believers need to invade digital space, just as Christians have always done, eager to use the latest developments in communication, whether it be ink on parchment, the printing press or radio and television. We've always known it's important not to be left behind. Fortunately there are people of faith blogging, tweeting, podcasting, posting on YouTube and designing websites for every group imaginable. It's good to see several excellent websites for daily prayer and reflection.[4] Worship and talks are 'streamed' live, and there has been an explosion of educational possibilities. But are we taking sufficient advantage of these opportunities?

- Because there's so much misuse of the internet, with bullying and abuse so common, Christians have an opportunity to stand out as those who write and post with care and have a different standard of online behaviour. Behind each tweet, blog or Facebook entry is a real person with real needs, reading those words. Hasty, two-dimensional ways of expressing thoughts and ideas can be immensely hurtful, and Christians will want to write responsibly and graciously, after the manner of Christ.

- We ought to be able to speak of our faith and the way we try to follow Jesus as naturally online as in person. This is no time or place to be shy about the spiritual dynamics of our lives, even if we risk some pretty bruising responses from those working out their pain and prejudice under cyber cover. Faith must have its place in this digital world, spoken with clarity, conviction and care. We have a faith to be proud of (even if we find that 'church' sometimes presents problems).

- As churches we may need to rethink our communication strategies. It's so easy to go online for information. People under 35 hardly ever think of print media; they think internet. Our websites therefore need to be full of useful, up-to-date, navigable information, with links to other sites and attractive visuals. Old information about past events gives out a sorrier message than out-of-date posters outside a church. Nevertheless, we mustn't forget that many older people come to church and still rely on print media. They mustn't be made to feel even more left behind. Again, all communication is a form of pastoral care. Indeed, churches could look out for older people disadvantaged by inability to use the internet. Basic computer classes or one-to-one guidance can be a real service.

- Lastly, we need to keep up. Every church needs someone with expertise to be a fixer or consultant in this brave new world. Perhaps a church needs a geeks group! And such people are usually passionate about their subject. They will tell us that Christians, like the rest of the population, spend large quantities of time online but that this everyday reality of the internet is hardly ever mentioned in the pulpit. Sermons are supposed to help us bring our faith to bear on issues of daily discipleship, and it should follow that they help us to work and play responsibly online, and how to be present there in distinctive Christian ways. Encourage your minister!

They said this

I think there is a world market for maybe five computers.

(Thomas Watson, chairman of IBM, 1943)

Computers in the future may weigh no more than 1.5 tons.
(*Popular Mechanics* magazine, 1949)

There is no reason anyone would want a computer in their home.
(Ken Olson, president of Digital Equipment Corp., 1977)

Taking it further

Anchor passage: John 1.1–14
Read once, take a full two minutes to reflect, then read it again.

To think about

Opener: What's your experience of living in an online world?

- 'In the beginning was the Word' (v. 1). How 'solid' does the idea of the Word/word remain in a digital age?
- What does the Word being 'full of grace and truth' mean to you (v. 14)? Can modern forms of communication be graceful and truthful?
- Are the internet and social networks controllable? Should they be?
- Do you agree with the ideas in 'What could we do differently?' above?

Prayer: Bring in a laptop and visit the site <www.sacredspace.ie> or <www.londoninternetchurch.org.uk> and explore what's available. Choose some part of one of the sites (or decide beforehand) and use that for prayer.

20

Worrying about religion

In 1762 the Scottish philosopher David Hume was at dinner in France and presumed to say that he doubted that there were any real atheists in the world. His host said: 'Look around you and count the guests.' There were 18 at the table. 'I can show you 15 atheists right off. The other three haven't made up their minds yet.'[1] Just over a century later Friedrich Nietzsche clinched the matter. 'God is dead,' he declared. 'God remains dead. And we have killed him.'[2]

Unfortunately nobody told God. In the early years of the twenty-first century the question of religion is more clearly on the agenda than ever. *God is Back* is the title of a book by the editor of *The Economist* and the chief of its Washington bureau, thus catching up with the 70–80 per cent of the world's population who never thought God had gone away.[3] But religion is a highly contested category. It's impossible not to worry about the place and impact of religion in the modern world. How should a follower of Jesus Christ view these questions?

What's the problem?

Put simply, religion is viewed by many as destructive, immoral or untrue – or maybe all three. Antagonists point to the self-declared religious motivation of the 9/11 terrorists in the United States and the 7/7 terrorists in

London. The intervention of the West in Iraq and Afghanistan is interpreted by many as a clash of civilizations, which also erupts in other places such as Nigeria, Pakistan and Sudan. Orthodox Jewish settlers in the West Bank are the cause of bitter Palestinian protests. In Sri Lanka Buddhism helped to fuel the bloody conflict with Hindu Tamils. In India and Pakistan, Muslim and Hindu violence makes a recurrent news story. Religion stoked the killing of a Dutch film-maker, the fatwa against Salman Rushdie and the violence that followed the publication of Danish cartoons of Mohammed. Everywhere it seems that religion is contentious.

Not only is religion seen as destructive, it's often now seen as immoral. The plight of women in many religions is regarded with horror by many Westerners, who will also cite the Church of England as guilty for a long time of an unholy mess over the acceptance of women bishops as equal to male bishops. In an age impatient with anything that smacks of discrimination, the Church's ambivalence over homosexuality causes disbelief and outrage in metropolitan wine bars. Even its commitment to the preservation of the environment is put into a context of what is seen as centuries of systematic abuse of the earth legitimized by the command in Genesis to 'fill the earth and subdue it' (Genesis 1.28). Instead of being the moral conscience of the nation, the suspicion has grown that religion is a deeply regressive force in society. In Britain, in many ways, the Church has lost the respect of the nation.

If religion is destructive and immoral, the final nail in its coffin is that it's also untrue. The Four Horsemen of the Apocalypse, Messrs Dawkins, Hitchens, Harris and Dennett, have had a field day demonstrating the ridiculous nature of religious truth-claims. Not for them the voices of subtle debate or the call of postmodernity for equal space in the field of ideas. Why argue with profound religious thinkers when there is the straw man of invincible fundamentalism to maul? Religion is rubbish. It's obvious.

How could we think about this?

Of course religion is fallible. It's the receptacle we use to carry our faith, and like any human construct, no matter how faith-full the intention of the designers, it's inevitably vulnerable to human folly. It's a familiar line, but if we find a perfect church none of us should join it, because we'd ruin it. That's the way we are. On the other hand, T. S. Eliot warned: 'If you will not have God, you should pay your respects to Hitler or Stalin.'[4] You could add Cambodia, Rwanda, Congo and others – none of these slaughters invoked God. There is certainly both healthy and unhealthy religion in our world, but the alternatives have equally negative qualities, with very few of the sublime gifts of religion.

Those gifts are ones in which the media doesn't seem to take much interest. The fact that every day millions of loving, caring and generous actions are performed by people of faith precisely because they are motivated by that faith is one that passes us by unless we experience it ourselves. This is one reason why local newspapers are much more open to good-news stories than the nationals: they see it happening. At local level the church is much more appreciated for what it does than at national level, where the predetermined script is of relentless decline, hypocrisy and failure. The local story is different. People usually experience their local church as a place of compassion and practical help. Rowan Williams said in an interview: 'My faith is one which tells me everybody is worth whatever time, attention and love you can possibly give.'[5] That's what millions of Christians give every day.

Religious faith has probably been the prime motivator for fundamental change in society. Where else can a major social and cultural change find its energy? When slavery was abolished, when the Factory Acts were needed, when prison reform had to overcome inertia, when housing, mental health and education needed structural reform, when racial segregation and apartheid needed to be swept away, when communism had to go – in every case it was religious faith that provided the mental and emotional fuel that reformers needed. Jonathan Porritt once put it to an audience in Oxford that the great faith traditions were essential in tackling the scale of the challenge of climate change. Society has the facts, the technology and the urgency; what we lack is life-changing energy, and that's the domain of faith.

If we're feeling particularly iconoclastic about religion we might bring Jesus to the witness stand. He was both a loyal Jew and a profound critic of the religious practices that he saw around him. He tore into religious hierarchies and restrictive practices, appalled by the strictures of religious machinery that could chew people up. Matthew 23 leaves us gasping for air. 'Woe to you, scribes and Pharisees, hypocrites, blind guides, snakes, brood of vipers' – Jesus was far more savage with religious systems than with, say, sexual sinners or fraudsters, as he tried to call them back to the core of their faith. If Jesus identified the problem so starkly, who are we to deny it? But then who are we to repeat it? Duly warned, we can do better.

When it comes to the charge that religion is basically untrue, there's need for much greater understanding of our faith, so that we can commend our beliefs with confidence. But at the same time we can rest assured that God doesn't actually need defending, any more than a Himalayan mountain, a lion in the wild or a mighty ocean needs defending. They simply are. We may argue about them as we wish but they have their own irrefutable existence against which human arguments fall like peas shot against the sky. In any case the intellectual steam has run out of so many of the reductionist arguments offered by the new atheists. A deeper, more respectful engagement is needed around these most profound issues.

———————

☆ *A young boy went bike-riding out into the country. He didn't pack any lunch, thinking he'd get something along the way. He had cycled many miles and was suffering hunger pangs when he arrived in a small village. He spied, outside a shop, a sign which had a picture of a filled roll. It looked magnificent, with salami and cheese, tomato and pickles. His mouth already began to water as he stepped up to the counter.*

'I'd like one of those rolls,' he said to the shopkeeper. The man looked puzzled for a few seconds, and then laughed.

'This isn't a food shop,' he said. 'We just paint signs.'

(It isn't signs people want from religion; it's the reality they point to.)[6]

———————

What could we do differently?

- As Christian disciples following the way of Jesus, our first instinct must always be to focus on God, front and centre, and to let the religious scaffolding follow. Religion is as important to faith as marriage is to love. It provides a vehicle for the handing on of faith, and a continuing shape to hold it. But the essence of Christianity is a lively faith in a loving God, and it is to God that we return our gaze daily, hourly, moment by moment, in order to get and keep our bearings in a turbulent world.

- We should also be people with a quiet confidence in the project on which we are embarked. The future shape of the Church is less important than the future reality of the kingdom of God, which is simply unstoppable. What Jesus has inaugurated isn't an idea that might run out of steam or go out of fashion. It's the irresistible triumph of love in every corner of life. What the Church will look like at the coming of the kingdom, I have no idea. I doubt that the Church of England is in the game plan, but some form of religious–spiritual body will still be faithful to the vision, as has always been the case. Relax; God knows the destination.

- We can continue to commit ourselves to the life of the church, even in bad times. When religious institutions are having a testing time, that's when they particularly need friends. You never give up on your family, and when dealing with church it's best to 'think family' rather than to 'think institution'. Don't walk out in a huff because they've changed the Communion wine or the time of the morning service, or even because the bishop has said something silly (*especially* if the bishop has said something silly, which he might well do). Each of us is a gift, to God, to the church, to each other. In our 'must-fit-me-precisely' culture we're used to everything being customized to our needs. But perhaps we're not the defining centre of everything. In which case, with humility, let's stay with God's people and make the church a truer reflection of the character of God.

- If we are worried about religion and the negative impact it can have on society, one response is to learn more and go deeper. It's easy to accept second-hand opinions pedalled by those who have made a life out of negativity. The great religious traditions each have an ocean of wisdom of which most of us know only a thimbleful. As world citizens we could do with learning more about the riches of, for example, Islam, Hinduism, Buddhism, Judaism. The Christian tradition is an extraordinary resource of spiritual riches, theological fascination, practical wisdom and human sanctity. We may enjoy fishing in other rivers but the Christian river is deep, wide and rich. If only more of the followers of Jesus understood the offer he makes! I'm always fascinated by the lengths people will go to in order to master a new skill. My wife has taken up pottery. Suddenly, we're the proud possessors of a wheel, several books on pottery, membership of a pottery class, and more. Learning is a committed business, and the rewards are wonderful. So too with our faith. If it's important, then it's important enough to learn more.

They said this

Of course, religious faith has a bad press in a secular society:
we unbelievers easily conflate it with fanaticism: faith, we think,
would be all right if it kept itself to itself and remained entirely
voluntary, like rubber fetishism, but it will insist on making converts,
attacking other faiths and generally behaving at once loutishly and
superciliously. And then there's the past, faith has baggage, whole
Terminal 5s of it. War, persecutions, pogroms – and the repression
of all forms of enlightenment.   (Will Self)[7]

When I mention religion I mean the Christian religion; and not
only the Christian religion but the Protestant religion; and not only
the Protestant religion but the Church of England.
                        (Henry Fielding's Parson Thwackum in *Tom Jones*)

Religion as a dull habit is not that for which Christ died.

(Thomas Kelly)[8]

Taking it further

Anchor passage: Isaiah 58.1–9a
Read once, take a full two minutes to reflect, then read it again.

To think about
Opener: How do you find your friends and neighbours speaking and thinking about religion these days? Any examples?

- 'Look, you serve your own interest' (v. 3). Do you see religions generally, and Christianity in particular, serving their own interest?
- 'Is not this the fast that I choose: to loose the bonds of injustice, to undo the thongs of the yoke, to let the oppressed go free . . . ?' (v. 6). How does your church do this?
- Have you been tempted to leave the church? Why? What did you do?
- 'If it's important, then it's important enough to learn more.' How do you try to learn more and what would you like to learn more about?

Prayer: Produce a map of the area you live in. Identify together on the map the various religious groups in your neighbourhood – in towns and cities that may be a number of different religions as well as Christian denominations; in rural areas it's more likely to be Christian churches. Decide who will pray for each group, asking that they will live up to the highest values of their faith. Then pray. And promise to pray during the coming week too.

21

Facing death

————◦•◆•◦————

'It's a funny old world. It's a lucky man who gets out of it alive.' So said the inimitable W. C. Fields. I happen to be writing this just after the death of a very special friend, one who had reached a stage beyond the precarious realm of emotions, and had handed herself over completely, body and soul, to the God who had loved and sustained her through all her many days. A highly intelligent woman, she approached death with simple clarity, in sure and certain hope of a future life with God. But not everyone is so confident.

What's the problem?

Facing death is the last great challenge for every person who has ever lived. The inevitability of death, approaching as a dark wind blowing from the future, is an awesome anticipation for everyone. As Julian Barnes says: 'Death never lets you down, remains on call seven days a week, and is happy to work three consecutive eight-hour shifts. You would buy shares in death if they were available; you would bet on it.'[1] Such certainty is never less than a serious challenge.

The danger is that the anticipation of death can blight the present. In Mark Haddon's novel, *A Spot of Bother*, George was watching a programme on television and suddenly had a moment of stark realization:

Someone unscrewed a panel in the side of George's head, reached in and tore out a handful of very important wiring. He felt violently ill. Sweat was pouring from beneath his hair and from the backs of his hands. He was going to die. Maybe not this month. Maybe not this year. But somehow, at some time, in a manner and at a speed very much not of his choosing. The floor seemed to have vanished to reveal a vast open shaft beneath the living room. With blinding clarity he realised he was frolicking in a summer meadow surrounded by a dark and impenetrable forest, waiting for that grim day on which they were dragged into the dark beyond the trees and individually butchered. How in God's name had he not noticed this before? And how did others not notice? Why did one not find them curled on the pavement howling? How did they saunter through their days unaware of this indigestible fact? And how, once the truth had dawned, was it possible to forget?[2]

Fear of the nature of death, whether it be sudden and sharp, or prolonged and difficult, is another cause of deep concern. Our expectations of the causes of death have changed considerably from a time when the register of deaths in Lamplugh parish for the years 1658–63 could disclose that three people were frightened to death by fairies, four were bewitched, three women were drowned on being tried for witchcraft and one was 'led into a horse pond by a will o'the wisp'. But anxiety remains. Fifty per cent of deaths are sudden, 20 per cent are prolonged. Two-thirds of deaths occur in hospital and a quarter at home, but the abiding uncertainty is about how we'll cope with physical pain, emotional distress and loss of dignity.

How could we think about this?

Reason battles to control the range of untidy emotions that the prospect of death evokes. The Christian faith has been consistent in its confidence in a future life beyond the confines of this one brief flicker of human time, but this possibility is denied by some and doubted by many. Philosopher Bertrand Russell wrote: 'There is darkness without and when I die there will be darkness within. There is no splendour, no vastness anywhere, only triviality for a moment and then nothing.'[3] This grim assessment is now probably the default position of large swathes of the British population, but it fades into a small minority view when put on to the world stage, where all the great religious traditions subscribe to some version of continuity or new life.

Christians, theoretically at any rate, don't believe in continuity, as if the soul lives on after the body has died. They believe in resurrection, a new life, a 'spiritual body' raised from the utter deadness of the grave. Greek dualism is not part of the Jewish–Christian world view. Paul fought hard to express what is inevitably mysterious when he wrote of the human body being 'sown a physical body' and 'raised a spiritual body' (1 Corinthians 15.44). Just as with a seed in the field, 'what you sow does not come to life unless it [first] dies' (v. 36). Christians base their confidence on the unique and unrepeatable event of the resurrection of Jesus, which completely reversed the tragic narrative of crucifixion and replaced it with a narrative of irrepressible life. While Jesus may or may not have been aware that this is what would happen to him, he had consistently spoken of the heavenly banquet as the trajectory and goal of our lives. Now he had broken through into this new order of being, and 'opened for us the gate of glory'.[4]

Although this is the nature of Christian belief, it doesn't follow that churchgoers in the West, living under the constant acid drip of secular assumptions, necessarily keep that belief on their list of 'definites'. There is a considerable degree of agnosticism on the afterlife in the average British churchgoer. Nevertheless, resurrection life is a core component of Christian belief.

> If there is no resurrection of the dead, then Christ has not been raised, and if Christ has not been raised, then our proclamation has been in vain . . . If for this life only we have hoped in Christ, we are of all people most to be pitied. (1 Corinthians 15.13, 19)

Perhaps the real question isn't the certainty of a new life in God, but the nature of that new life. Anthropocentric pictures of heaven as a continuity of life in bourgeois Britain but with the bumps smoothed out simply won't do. But nor will absorption into the Absolute. In between is, perhaps, a life in which we have a distinct, fulfilled identity in which the best that we have been is brought to completion. It's said that you can't take it with you when you go, but the only thing we could take with us anyway is the only thing we ever really had – and that's the love of God. It's in that love that we trust.

We can also believe that a God of love and justice will not let sorrow last. Our belief in the value of truth, justice, love, mercy, compassion and so on only makes sense in the context of absolutes of which our present experiences are but shadows. So there will be a new heaven and a new earth, for the first heaven and the first earth will have passed away (Revelation 21.1). And here the compassion of God will be overwhelming: 'He will wipe every tear from their eyes. Death will be no more; mourning and crying and pain will be no more, for the first things have passed away' (v. 4). And Christians, who have a suffering Lord at the heart of their faith, know that the last tears God will wipe away will be his own.

☆ *A well-known rake was found on his deathbed by a friend, with the Bible in one hand and a whisky in the other. 'Why are you reading the Bible?' the friend asked. 'I'm looking for a loophole,' came the answer.*

What could we do differently?

• Faced with such a 'life-changing' event, we might spend time working through it in advance. A wonderful, intelligent friend wrote this as he looked ahead:

> Having cancer disrupted my sense of the continuity of life. I have had to adjust to the prospect of not living to be 60 rather than living to 85 like most of my family. However, after much struggling, I have come to accept it and to set myself to 'redeem the time' that is left.

I am engaged with fulfilling projects at work and spending a lot of time with old friends, re-living the past with enjoyment and gratitude. I have reviewed the achievements and failures of my life and handed them over to God. My faith in Christ who passed through death and overcame it gives me hope not just for the next life but for life here and now. My conviction that nothing can separate us from the eternal purposes of God for our good has survived the test of living with cancer. It enables me to live each day in thanksgiving and peace, leaving the future in those strong and compassionate hands.[5]

- Here was thoughtful, mature preparation that enabled him to let go with dignity and faith. One way of doing our own preparation, without knowing the date or time, is to try writing our own epitaph or obituary. (A monk playfully suggested for himself: 'Died peacefully in his bed, surrounded by two of his favourite wives.'[6]) What we write could be the person we'd like to be, and the question we're left with is: 'What's stopping me from being that person?' If that's what lies within me as my highest goal and desire, why don't I turn every effort to achieving that? This gives value and purpose to our days, whether they be few or many. Facing death is then a springboard to life.
- It must be part of our discipleship to help others handle death. There's a lot of death around, whether it be on the news, in the neighbourhood or among our friends. Some people shy away from it. Bereaved people know all too well the painful sight of people they know crossing the street when they see them coming, rather than having to handle the embarrassment (or infection?) of talking with them. We don't need to know what to say to a bereaved person; presence and touch are more important than words – and if a meal brought to the door can be added to the list, that's even better. And if we ourselves are unfortunately having to adjust to terminal illness, the greatest gift we can give to our loved ones is a good death, one in which we live fully in the present, remembering the past with gratitude and looking to the future with quiet assurance, neither fussing nor

understating. A good death requires patience and courage, and the handing over of our lives to the One who has loved us, and will love us, from eternity to eternity.

In 1983 David Nye was killed in a helicopter crash with his wife and three daughters. Shortly before, he had written the following in the Bank of England staff magazine:

☆ *The death of a relation, one dearly loved, focuses the thoughts on the inescapable movement forward to life. Such a sorrow forces home the realisation that our existence allows no escape from change, from the unexpected, from the whole realm of life's possibilities, from comedy to deepest tragedy. Experience dispels what one might call the Blandings Castle illusion, that perpetual Shropshire summer is humanly attainable. For even as the mallet swings and the croquet ball glides through the hoop into a patch of evening sunlight, in the midst of such domestic peace, time opens the crevasse at our feet. We none of us know, however secure behind the love of those around us, or bolstered by power and possessions, what even the next moment may mean to us. To imagine otherwise is to be, at the very least, unprepared.*

They said this

Death is the supreme festival on the road to freedom.
(Dietrich Bonhoeffer)[7]

Live as if you were going to die tomorrow. Die as if you were going to live forever. (St Ignatius Loyola)

The royal doors are opening! The Great Liturgy is about to begin.
(The dying words of Prince Eugene Trubetskoy)[8]

172

Taking it further

Anchor passage: 1 Corinthians 15.3–14, 20 (everyone should have their own copy of the text)
Explain that when the passage is read out everyone will be asked to identify one word or phrase that strikes them. Two minutes' silence will be given, and then these words or phrases will be shared, without any explanation. Then the passage will be read again, with a further two minutes' for reflection, after which everyone will be asked to say why they chose their phrase and what it means to them. Further discussion may follow. Having explained the process, try it out.

To think about
Opener: What does Easter mean to you? What are your best memories of Easter?

- Using your imagination, what do you think might have been behind v. 6 ('Then he appeared to more than five hundred brothers and sisters at one time')?
- 'He appeared also to me' (v. 8). How does that kind of appearance sit alongside the appearances of the risen Christ to the disciples/ apostles?
- 'If Christ has not been raised, then our proclamation has been in vain' (v. 14). How much leeway do you think there is in interpreting what actually happened in the resurrection?
- Does it surprise or worry you that many churchgoers are agnostic about life after death? How important is life after death to you?

Prayer: Go round the group naming a few members of our own hall of fame – the people to whom we owe most in our own faith but who have now died. Give thanks for them by name. Then each person says how they would like to be remembered themselves, following which each person prays for someone else in the group – that they should become as they would like to be remembered.

PS Enjoy life!

---◆◆◆---

'Enjoy!' she said, and seemed to mean it. She was serving us at the airport as we prepared to go off on holiday. It was many years ago now, but it was the first time this familiar *adieu* had been said to me. It struck me then that it's something Christians could say to each other a lot more often than we probably do.

Following Jesus in the dance of life is surely the best way of spending our days. The seventeenth-century Westminster Shorter Catechism said that 'Man's chief end is to glorify God and enjoy him forever.' That lovely phrase at least serves to counterbalance the suspicion many people seem to have that Christians are worried that someone, somewhere, might be enjoying themselves. If only they realized we're fundamentally committed to enjoyment – of God and of life itself. The phrase of Jesus that has meant most to me all my Christian life is: 'I have come that they may have life and have it abundantly' (John 10.10).

I was brought up in a wonderful Christian home but the faith itself was a kind of wallpaper which required little of me but a nodding acquaintance with God. There was a lot of 'God material' lying around but it had no wheel-nut to hold it together, no central piece of the Christian jigsaw. It was only when I went to university that I met a group of young people who had a spark and a depth to their faith that intrigued me, and who spoke of faith as a living relationship with Jesus Christ rather than as a dutiful fulfilment of rather tired instructions. For them, Christ was alive, and life was exciting. I put a toe in the water. Soon I dived in.

It still feels as if I've only put a toe in the divine life that floods the world. The scale of God's love in creation, in Christ and in our daily lives is something I continually underestimate – as I will always do, since it's God who will always embrace and enfold us, rather than the other way round. This is 'a love that will not let me go' and that seeks to give me as much as I can take without blowing a fuse. Enjoy God? Yes please!

There's another complementary bonus here as well, and that's the delightful fact that God wants to enjoy us too. We're told in Genesis that, having just made human beings, 'God saw everything that he had made, and indeed, it was very good' (Genesis 1.31). This is the enjoyment of a parent looking at her children playing in the sand and knowing that life has no greater joy. The mutual enjoyment of God, and those whom God has created, is an echo of the mutuality of the Trinity where the love of Father, Son and Holy Spirit swirls together in sheer delight.

How?

You don't usually have to tell a child how to enjoy herself. Just give her some sand, some sticks and stones, some grass, a ball, a little friend – anything – and she'll make up a wonderful game. As we grow older it seems that we forget some of that spontaneity and imagination, and teenage angst is followed by early-bird success anxiety, middle-aged status anxiety and later-life pension anxiety. Where has the child gone? Christian faith seeks to recover that primary relationship with God so that the hidden child can re-emerge and play in the safety of the Trinity. And Christian discipleship is then about enjoying life to the full by living in God's world, in God's way, with God's help.

This book has been about how to do that. It's about living faithfully. Living in God's way in the knockabout challenges of everyday life carries the deep satisfaction of going with the grain of God's life and energy, even if it makes us think and pray harder than we ever really wanted. There's both spiritual and intellectual pleasure in trying to align our thinking and actions with the mind of God. This alignment is what the disciple seeks in handling relationships, money, work, sexuality, ambition, temptation, politics, health, the environment, social networking – all the things touched on in the chapters of this book.

But there's so much more to enjoying life in God's good world.

- *For some people, fun is physical.* The London Olympics in 2012 demonstrated how much enthusiasm can be generated by sport, and drew us into the sheer exhilaration of being physical creatures. When my wife says she's tempted to take up volleyball, you know something serious has taken place. Pushing the body to its limits releases endorphins that give a profound enjoyment to exercise, but even a sedentary cleric knows the quiet joy of walking through a Lakeland valley on a summer's evening. We enjoy life at a very basic, visceral level through our bodies.
- *For many people, fun is cultural.* We don't need to be 'culture vultures,' hoovering up exhibitions, museums, plays and concerts at frenetic pace, to know that culture is one of the chief sources of profound enjoyment for a considerable proportion of the population. Art galleries are constantly surprised and delighted at the overwhelming success of their exhibitions. I tried to get tickets for one exhibition on the day it started its four-month run, but nothing was available for any day, at any time. Music can transport us to places too sublime to name. To be lost in a good book is a goal much sought after by very many of us. Poetry, pottery, paintings, all things artistic, can give us a deep-down smile of sheer satisfaction at something well formed, something true.
- *For yet others, fun is travelling.* The joy of experiencing a new place in a new time zone, new people with fresh festivals, new conversations over new drinks – these are the stimuli we love and that keep us glued to the travel magazines. It's like the amazement of the sinner in heaven – 'so much I never knew'. I travel endlessly in my head, imagining the fascination of different cultures, planning the places I could visit and photograph. But then there are the bins to put out . . .

One of the most important places for me, and the focus of a lifetime's obsession, is mountains. I climb them (more so in the past), read about them, photograph them, buy maps of them. I've trekked in the Himalayas; I've done the Three Peaks Challenge; I've climbed Mount Sinai before dawn. I've been to the Lake District almost every year of my life. I've clung to Striding Edge in a gale, drenched and decidedly alarmed. I've swung down into Great Langdale after a day on the fells, tired, sunburnt and eager for that welcoming pint. I've made for the mountains whenever I've been given a sniff of a chance. I've refused a good job because there was no land anywhere I could see over 50 ft. And I've felt more at one with my Maker and Redeemer on a mountain top than almost anywhere else I've ever been. Do you have anything you enjoy like that? God meets us in our joy and smiles at our pleasure.

There are, in other words, so many different ways of framing the idea of 'enjoying life', but all of them are immensely enriched by letting faith permeate them. What we are exploring, touching, tasting, creating and so on, are different aspects of a God of such breath-taking inventiveness and grace it's beyond imagining. But God's world is all there for the enjoying.

Bear Grylls is an adventurer who loves the wild outdoors with a passion. While still young he climbed Everest. This is what he wrote about the start of the final 17-hour day in what's called the Death Zone.

☆ *7 p.m. Half an hour to go until we started the laborious task of getting kitted up again. It would take us at least an hour. By the end no part of our bodies or faces would be visible. We would be transformed into cocooned figures, huddled, awaiting our fate. I reached into the top pouch of my backpack and pulled out a few crumpled pages wrapped in plastic. I had brought them just for this moment. 'Even the youths shall faint and be weary, and the young men shall utterly fall. But those who wait upon the Lord shall renew their strength. They shall mount up with wings like eagles. They shall run and not be weary. They shall walk and not faint' (Isaiah 40.29–31). I felt that this was all I really had up here. There's no one else with enough extra strength to keep you safe. It really is just you and your Maker. No pretence, no fluff – no plan B. Over the next twenty-four hours there would be a one in six chance of dying. That focuses the mind. And the bigger picture becomes important. It was time to look death in the eye. Time to acknowledge that fear, hold the hand of the Almighty, and climb on. And those simple Bible verses would ring round my head for the next night and day, as we pushed on ever higher.*[1]

Bear Grylls has a passionate commitment to living at full stretch; life in all its fullness. His approach might encourage us to ask how passionately we go about enjoying life as God's gift. Christian discipleship is a kind of extreme sport. Not everyone does it; some think it's eccentric; but to those who have encountered Christ there's nothing more interesting, rewarding and right to do with our lives. This is what we were made for – to live in God's world, in God's way, with God's help.

At the last judgement it's said that God will ask us a single question: 'Did you enjoy my creation?' With all my heart I want to be able to say: 'Yes Lord, I did!'

Notes

The case for the prosecution

1 Alfred North Whitehead, *Religion in the Making* (New York, Meridian Books, 1960), p. 16.
2 C. S. Lewis, 'Is theology poetry?', *The Weight of Glory: And other addresses* (New York, Harper Collins, 1980), p. 140.
3 An image used by Mark Greene in the work of the London Institute for Contemporary Christianity, <www.licc.org.uk>.
4 Robert Putnam, *Bowling Alone* (New York, Simon & Schuster, 2001).
5 Robert Putnam and David Campbell, *American Grace* (New York, Simon & Schuster, 2010).
6 Jonathan Sacks, *Standpoint* magazine, January/February 2012.
7 Eugene Peterson, *A Long Obedience in the Same Direction* (Downers Grove, Illinois, IVP, 2000).
8 G. K. Chesterton, from his introduction to *The Book of Job* (London, Wellman, 1907).
9 Alan Hargrave, *Living Well* (London, SPCK, 2010), p. 103.

Part 1: Facing God

1 William Temple, *Readings in St John's Gospel* (London, Macmillan, 1963).
2 Simone Weil, *Waiting for God* (New York, HarperCollins, 2001), pp. 26–7.
3 Rowan Williams, *Tokens of Trust* (Norwich, Canterbury Press, 2007), p. 60.

1 Living gracefully

1 Tom Wright, *For All God's Worth* (London, SPCK, 1997).
2 HM The Queen, *BBC News*, June 2012.

2 Knowing God's guidance

1 Ken Costa, *God at Work* (London, Continuum, 2007), p. 60.
2 <www.quotationspage.com/quote/40.html>.

3 Handling money

1 Greg Smith, *Evening Standard*, 14 March 2012.
2 Paul Morrison, *It's Time to Close the Gap* (London, Church Action on Poverty, 2012), p. 9.
3 One Society, *A Third of a Percent* (London, One Society, 2011).
4 Tim Jackson, *Prosperity Without Growth* (London, Earthscan, 2009).
5 *The Week*, 12 May 2012.
6 Sam Wells, *Be Not Afraid* (Grand Rapids, Baker, 2011), p. 92.

4 Handling our sexuality

1 *Sunday Times*, 10 January 2010.
2 <www.brook.org.uk>.
3 Office for National Statistics, *Social Trends* (London, ONS, 2000).
4 Book of Common Prayer.
5 Peter Owen Jones, *Bed of Nails* (Oxford, Lion, 1997), p. 181.
6 Martin Luther, <www.brainyquote.com>.

5 Facing temptation

1 Office of National Statistics, 2011.
2 John Roberts, CNN, 28 July 2010.
3 *Psychologies* magazine, 2010.
4 Professor Gail Dines, CNN, 28 July 2010.
5 Office of National Statistics, 2011.
6 Government's Gambling Commission, 2010.
7 <www.wikipedia.org>.
8 <www.addictedtomore.com/alcohol>.

6 Being healthy

1 <www.livebelowtheline.org.uk>, part of the Global Poverty Project.
2 Quoted in Christine Craggs-Hinton, *Coping with Eating Disorders and Body Image* (London, Sheldon, 2006), p. 3.
3 Information supplied by Anglican Health Network.
4 Cancer Research UK, *The House Magazine*, 5 July 2012.
5 <www.templeton.org>.
6 <www.stmarylebone.org>.

7 Working faithfully

1 Krish Kandiah, *Twenty-four: Integrating faith and real life* (Milton Keynes, Authentic, 2007), p. 52.
2 Film, *Chariots of Fire*, 1981.
3 Mark Greene, *The Great Divide* (London, London Institute for Contemporary Christianity, 2010), p. 6.
4 Greene 2010, p. 22.
5 Ken Costa, *God at Work* (London, Continuum, 2007), p. 30.

8 Going shopping

1 Tom Bower, *Sweet Revenge: The intimate life of Simon Cowell* (London, Faber & Faber, 2012).
2 Susie Orbach, *Sunday Times*, 20 January 2002.
3 'China: Youth', *Time* magazine, 18 June 2012.
4 *Today* programme, BBC, 1 June 2012.
5 'Greener by miles', *Daily Telegraph*, 3 June 2007.
6 Guy Brandon, *Free to Live* (London, SPCK, 2010), p. 60.
7 'FINE' is an acronym for an association of the four largest fair trade networks.
8 Alison Morgan, *The Wild Gospel* (Oxford, Monarch, 2004), p. 171.
9 Erich Fromm, *The Art of Loving* (London, Thorsons, 2010; originally published 1956), p. 60.

9 Being political

1 David Cameron, speech on King James Bible, 8 December 2011, Christ Church Cathedral, Oxford.
2 Barack Obama, *Dreams from my Father* (Edinburgh, Canongate, 2007).
3 Charles Elliot, *Praying through Paradox* (London, Fount, 1987), p. 53.
4 Helder Camara, quoted in Z. Rocha, *Helder, o dom* (Brazil, Editora Vozes, 2000), p. 53.
5 Tony Blair, *New Statesman*, March 2009.
6 Jim Wallis, *Faith Works* (London, SPCK, 2002), p. 184.

10 Making peace

1 <www.womensaid.org.uk>.
2 Chris Hedges, *War is a Force that Gives Us Meaning* (New York, Public Affairs, 2002), p. 13.
3 Desmond Tutu, <commondreams.org/views06/0913-22.htm>.
4 Brian McLaren, *Everything Must Change* (Nashville, Thomas Nelson, 2007), p. 154.
5 Jonathan Swift, <www.thinkexist.com>.

6 Robert Runcie when Archbishop of Canterbury, 1981.
7 Tertullian, *Apologetics* 39.
8 Based on the story in Rowan Williams and Joan Chittister, *For All That Has Been, Thanks* (Norwich, Canterbury Press, 2010), p. 123.
9 McLaren 2007, p. 161.
10 Martin Luther King Jr, as quoted in Stephen B. Oates, *Let the Trumpet Sound* (New York, Harper & Row, 1982).

11 Doing justice

1 United Nations report of the World Institute for Economic Development Research, *The Guardian*, 6 December 2006.
2 <www.oneworld.net/article/view/144146/1/3319>.
3 Richard Wilkinson and Kate Pickett, *The Spirit Level* (London, Penguin, 2009).
4 *The Freedom Bible* (Swindon, Bible Society, 2010).
5 Richard Rohr, *Preparing for Christmas* (Cincinnati, St Anthony Messenger Press, 2008).
6 R. S. Thomas, *Later Poems* (London, Macmillan, 1983), p. 35.
7 John Ruskin, *The Crown of the Wild Olive* (London, Allen & Unwin, 1915), Lecture 1.3.
8 Lionel Blue speaking at the Faithlit Festival, Bloxham, October 2011.
9 In James Brett (ed.), *Abraham Kuyper: A Centennial Reader* (Grand Rapids, Eerdmans, 1998), p. 461.
10 John V. Taylor, *The Easter God* (London, Continuum, 2003), p. 117.

12 Being attentive

1 Judy Hirst, *Struggling to be Holy* (London, Darton, Longman and Todd, 2006), p. 73.

13 Being married

1 *Daily Telegraph*, 8 December 2011.
2 *BBC News*, 4 October 2007.
3 <www.civitas.org.uk/hwu/cohabitation>.
4 Petru Dumitriu, *Incognito* (London, Collins, 1964).
5 Shakespeare, Sonnet 116.

14 Nurturing friendships

1 C. S. Lewis, *The Four Loves* (London, Geoffrey Bles, 1960), p. 77.
2 A. A. Milne, *The House at Pooh Corner* (London, Methuen, first published 1928).

3 Attributed to Albert Camus but unconfirmed.
4 Henri Nouwen, *The Road to Daybreak* (London, Darton, Longman and Todd, 1989).
5 Jon Katz, <www.goodreads.com/quotes/tag/friendship>.

15 Building community

1 William Paul Young, *The Shack* (London, Hodder & Stoughton, 2007).
2 Roy Searle, Church Army AGM, 2010.
3 Brother Sam SSF, *Transmission*, magazine of the Bible Society, Spring 1998.
4 Victor Turner, *The Ritual Process* (Chicago, Aldine, 1969).
5 Alasdair MacIntyre, *After Virtue* (London, Duckworth, 1981), p. 263.

16 Sharing faith

1 See Peter Ball and Malcolm Grundy, *Faith on the Way: A practical parish guide to the adult catechumenate* (London, Mowbray, 2000).
2 An Anglican initiative that has proved popular and effective in encouraging churches to invite people who have fallen out of the habit of churchgoing to come and see; <www.backtochurch.co.uk>.

17 Handling future shock

1 Peggy Noonan, writing in 1998.
2 Martin Rees, *Our Final Century* (London, Arrow, 2003), p. 8.
3 A word used by Alvin Toffler, *Future Shock* (London, Pan, 1973).
4 Julian of Norwich, *Revelations of Divine Love*, various translations and publishers.
5 Michael Sadgrove, source unknown.
6 St Augustine, *The Confessions, Book XI, Time and Eternity*, various publishers.
7 Ken Costa, *God at Work* (London, Continuum, 2007), p. 156.

18 Loving the planet

1 John Guillebaud, *The Bible in Transmission* (London, Bible Society, 2006), p. 18.
2 *The Times*, 26 May 2009.
3 James Martin, *Oxford Today* magazine, 2011.
4 *The Guardian*, 28 January 2011.
5 James Martin, 2011.
6 Barry Commoner, *The Closing Circle: Confronting the environmental crisis* (New York, Bantam Books, 1980).
7 Gillian Straine and Nathan Oxley, *For Creed and Creation* (Oxford, Diocese of Oxford, 2011).

8 Alan Durning, *How Much is Enough? The Consumer Society and the Future of the Earth* (New York and London, W. W. Norton, 1992).
9 James Martin, 2011.

19 Living in an online world

1 Martin Rees, *Our Final Century* (London, Arrow, 2003), p. 15.
2 Robert Harris, *The Fear Index* (London, Arrow, 2012), postscript.
3 Peter Graystone, *Church Times*, 6 January 2012.
4 Search engines produce a number of sites, such as: <www.churchofengland.org/prayer>; the Jesuit site <www.sacredspace.ie>; and <www.londoninternetchurch.org.uk>.

20 Worrying about religion

1 Peter Gay, *The Enlightenment: The rise of modern paganism* (New York, Norton, 1966), p. 400.
2 Friedrich Nietzsche, *The Gay Science* (Cambridge, Cambridge University Press, 2001; originally published 1882).
3 John Micklethwait and Adrian Wooldridge, *God is Back* (London, Penguin, 2009).
4 T. S. Eliot, *The Idea of a Christian Society* (New York, Harcourt, Brace, 1940), p. 64.
5 Rowan Williams in the *Evening Standard*, 27 June 2012.
6 Mike Riddell, *Godzone* (Oxford, Lion, 1992), p. 74.
7 Will Self in *Harper's Bazaar*, November 2010.
8 Thomas Kelly, *A Testament of Devotion* (San Francisco, HarperCollins, 1992).

21 Facing death

1 Julian Barnes, *Nothing to be Frightened of* (London, Vintage, 2009), p. 70.
2 Mark Haddon, *A Spot of Bother* (London, Vintage, 2007), p. 90.
3 Bertrand Russell, *Autobiography, Vol. 2* (London, Allen & Unwin, 1968), p. 159.
4 Holy Communion, *Common Worship* (London, Church House Publishing, 2000).
5 Article in *Abingdon Parish Magazine* by Christopher Jones, 2011.
6 Sam Wells, *Be Not Afraid* (Grand Rapids, Brazos Press, 2011), p. 15.
7 Dietrich Bonhoeffer, *Letters and Papers from Prison* (London, SCM Press, 2001).
8 George Every, Richard Harries and Kallistos Ware (eds), *The Time of the Spirit: Readings through the Christian year* (New York, St Vladimir Seminary Press, 1984), p. 84.

PS Enjoy life!

1 Bear Grylls, *Mud, Sweat and Tears* (London, Channel 4 Books, 2011), p. 385.